To Gerry

Best Wishes for A Happy

Birthday.

Bob + Norma.   1989.

The
Mainly Microwave
Cookbook

The
Mainly Microwave
Cookbook

The art of combining microwave
and traditional cooking

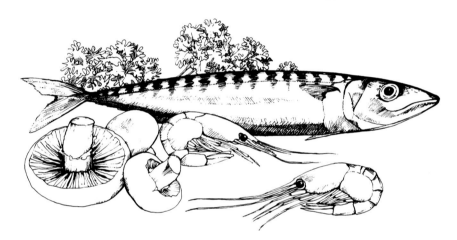

Rosemary Moon

DAVID & CHARLES
Newton Abbot   London   North Pomfret (Vt)

*This book is for Nick, despite the fact that
he's still slim at the end of it!*

————————————

(front cover) *Stuffed Salmon en Croûte with
Hollandaise Sauce (page 115), Courgettes with
Sesame Seeds (page 116), Cauliflower with Tomato
Sauce (page 116), Pâté du Maison (page 114),
Lemon Soufflé (page 116)*

(back cover) *see page 67*

(previous page) *left to right: Poppy Seed Rolls (page
97), Cheesy Granary Bread (page 94), Cottage Milk
Loaf (page 97), Light Rye Rolls (page 96), Light Rye
Bread Plait (page 96), Wholewheat Bread (page 2)*

British Library Cataloguing in Publication Data
Moon, Rosemary
 The mainly microwave cookbook: the art
 of combining microwave and traditional
 cooking.
 1. Microwave cookery
 I. Title
 641.5′882   TX832

 ISBN 0-7153-8916-5

Phototypeset by Typesetters (Birmingham) Ltd,
Smethwick, West Midlands
and printed in West Germany
by Mohndruck GmbH
for David & Charles Publishers plc
Brunel House   Newton Abbot   Devon

Published in the United States of America
by David & Charles Inc
North Pomfret   Vermont 05053   USA

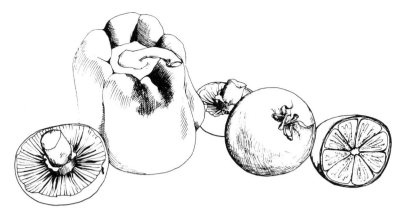

Contents

Acknowledgements

Grateful thanks to:

CLARE HAYSOM, for help with the preparation of food for photography.

PANASONIC UK Ltd, for the loan of a microwave for some of the testing.

THE WEDGEWOOD ROOM, HANNINGTONS OF BRIGHTON, for the loan of china for photography.

JOHN PLIMMER, RPM PHOTOGRAPHIC, Havant, Hants; special thanks for all the thought and planning.

The staff of RPM PHOTOGRAPHIC, for their interest, cups of tea, and for kindly eating much of the photographed food!

PAT MacCARTHY for the line illustrations.

Introduction

The microwave cooker is becoming more and more widely used. Many cookers are bought for the initial purposes of defrosting and reheating, but are soon in use for cooking a great variety of foods. Experienced microwave users seldom cook fish or vegetables by any other method and view their cookers as a very valuable addition to their standard kitchen equipment – the conventional cooker with grill, the refrigerator, the freezer and, in many cases, the pressure cooker.

Microwave cookers will cook anything – in as much as they will heat it up! However, just as with conventional methods of cooking one would choose to cook a rib of beef in the oven rather than in a pan of water, and brussels sprouts on the hob rather than under the grill, so the decision has to be made as to what is best cooked in the microwave and what should be cooked by more traditional methods.

When preparing complete meals, especially for upwards of four people, it is necessary to use a second method of cooking, in addition to the microwave, if all the components of the meal are to be ready and hot at the same time. Meals cooked completely by microwave tend to involve a lengthy process of reheating prior to serving.

The recipes in this book are for mainly microwave cookery, in as much as many of them require at least a second cooking appliance, be it a hob, oven, freezer or pressure cooker. This proves very useful in the preparation of meals as it allows time for other dishes to be cooked in the microwave when the second cooking appliance is in use. Special emphasis is given to the serving of complete meals, with ideas for accompanying vegetables and, in some cases, complete menus.

Much initial knowledge regarding the use of microwave cookers can be gained from manufacturers' instruction/recipe books, or the many excellent microwave cookbooks that are available through bookshops. Detailed charts for defrosting foods and cooking meats, fruits and vegetables will be found in these publications.

Basic rules for microwave cookery

There are a few basic rules that must be understood if the best possible use is to be made of the microwave cooker.

* *Microwaves do not cook food from the inside outwards!* They penetrate into the food to a depth of up to 4cm/1½in, and the heat then conducts to the centre of the food, in exactly the same way as in the conventional oven. When cooking on 100% or full power, it is therefore important to stir foods half way through cooking to get even heating.

* The general rule for when to cover foods is: if you would cover for conventional cooking, cover it in the microwave.

* If you wish to double the quantities in a recipe, add approximately half as much cooking time again.

* If you wish to halve the quantities in a recipe, take off approximately one third of the cooking time.

* Always have a look at the food before the end of the suggested cooking time – you can easily add extra time but you can never take it away once the food is overcooked.

Variable power control

It is unthinkable that one would purchase a gas or conventional electric cooker that only had one heat setting – fruit cakes are not at their best when cooked at gas mark 9 or 250°C/500°F!

The first microwave cookers had only one setting – on. It was quickly found that resting or standing times had to be included in the cooking period to allow the heat to spread evenly throughout the food.

Microwave cookers usually now have at least four power settings, allowing for gentle heating of more delicate foods. One setting is often labelled defrost for the purpose of thawing frozen foods. This setting can, however, also be used for cooking, and is especially useful for casseroles.

Variable power is achieved in two ways, either by automatically combining periods of pulsed microwave energy with standing periods, or by using a continuous low power, eg 300W instead of 650W. I have found the first method to be the most effective as there should be no requirement for standing times which are already built in to the cooking time. With the continuous low power method, a standing time of 5–10min at the end of the cooking period will still be required.

There is no standard terminology for microwave power levels, so they are referred to in these recipes as percentages. The following is a rough guide to the settings and their uses:

100% Full power, for general cooking. Unless otherwise stated, all recipes for the microwave should be cooked on 100%.

70% Used for cooking densely textured foods, eg joints of red meat and foods that cannot be stirred, eg large dishes of lasagne. This setting is also used for reheating foods that cannot be stirred.

50% A moderate heat, used for simmering foods. This setting is also used to defrost foods with an open texture, eg breads, vegetable casseroles, etc.

30% Generally used for defrosting, but also invaluable for casseroles of red meat.

Using a pulsed variable power setting, I have found that it is generally not necessary to allow standing time at the end of a cooking period.

Standing time

Standing time was originally necessary to allow heat to spread evenly through large or dense foods. If variable power settings are used correctly there is no need to allow foods to stand at the end of their cooking period (see Variable Power Control, p7). The exceptions are for foods that would be allowed a standing period when cooked conventionally, eg rice and roast meats. Some microwave cooked cakes are allowed to stand for 5min before being turned out of their dishes – this is simply to allow them to set slightly before being cooled on a wire rack.

Defrosting in the microwave

Most microwave cookers have a defrost setting (see Variable Power, p7) which is at a fixed level. However, some manufacturers employ a sophisticated system whereby the machine automatically changes power levels as the food becomes more defrosted – so initial heating is at a high setting to start melting the ice, and a progressively lower setting is used as the food softens and defrosts. This system gives a very even thaw.

Some manufacturers employ an automatic system of weighing and then defrosting the food. This is most effective if the user has the ability to programme the microwave with the type of food that is to be defrosted. 450g/1lb steak requires a longer, more gentle defrosting period than 450g/1lb peas.

Many people think of the microwave cooker primarily for defrosting, and especially for joints of meat. For the fixed defrost setting I have found that it is better to give an initial defrosting period of 10–20min, depending on the size of the joint, and then to allow the joint to finish defrosting for 1–2hr at room temperature. Defrosting too rapidly will cause a loss of meat juices and a dry cooked result.

Defrosting times are given for each recipe, where applicable. These are intended as a guide only, as the operating temperature of your freezer will affect defrosting times.

Cooking vegetables

It is especially important to remember to stir vegetables half way through their cooking period (see Basic Rules for Microwave Cookery, p7). Some vegetables, especially those with a strong flavour, such as cauliflower and brussels sprouts, can be more palatable if boiled conventionally, but this is a matter of personal taste.

The basic rules for vegetable cooking are:

* Stir the vegetables half way through the cooking period.
* Add very little salt, and make sure that it is well mixed with the water used to cook the vegetables. Salt is a flavour enhancer, and less will be required when cooking by microwaves than for conventionally cooked foods.
* Some vegetables, especially when cooked in quantities sufficient for a family, may be cooked quicker on the hob. This should be considered when planning a meal.
* A vegetable that will keep warm without spoiling, eg Braised Red Cabbage (p109), should be cooked first, then placed in the conventional oven to keep warm while cooking the second vegetable in the microwave.

* Root vegetables generally require 7–8min per 450g/lb.

* Vegetables with thick stalks and delicate tips, eg asparagus and calabrese, should be arranged in a dish so that the stalks are towards the edge of the dish and the tips are in the centre. This will give an evenly cooked result.

Covering food in the microwave

Many foods do require covering during cooking (see Basic Rules for Microwave Cookery, p7). This helps them to cook more quickly by keeping a large amount of steam in the dish, and also keeps the food moist.

* Food that would be covered to be cooked conventionally should generally be covered in the microwave.

* Using a dish with a lid is the most convenient way of covering the food.

* Large microwave mixing bowls, covers or plates may also be used for covering dishes.

* Only use non-pvc film in the microwave cooker.

* Foods that may spatter, eg fish cooked in butter, or chicken, may be cooked covered with kitchen paper. This will prevent the microwave cooker from getting soiled but will allow the steam to escape, thus preventing a boiled flavour.

Reheating in the microwave

Foods to be reheated are generally covered and heated at 100% power. They should be stirred once or twice during heating. Foods that cannot be stirred, including plate meals, are best heated at 70% power.

These general hints cover the basic rules of good microwave cookery. Further tips are given throughout the book.

The microwave & the pressure cooker

The pressure cooker has been used in conjunction with the microwave for three or four recipes in this book. I have found that for quickly cooking the cheaper cuts of red meat, the pressure cooker gives a more tender result, in a shorter time than the microwave.

The recipes

The following recipes have all been tested in a 700W microwave cooker, and many have been retested at 600W. For cookers with a power output of 400–500W, it will be necessary to add 10–20% extra cooking time to that stated in the recipe.

Quantities are given in both metric and imperial measures throughout the book. Work from one set of measurements only, and do not mix metric and imperial quantities.

All eggs are size 4, unless otherwise stated.

Symbols

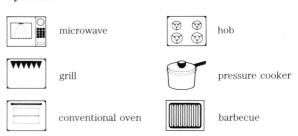

microwave   hob

grill   pressure cooker

conventional oven   barbecue

Soups & Snacks

The microwave cooker can speed the preparation of soups for the average family of four and can be used to soften vegetables before finishing cooking larger quantities in a saucepan on the hob. Where poultry or game carcasses are being cooked with dried pulse vegetables, the carcasses should be simmered on the hob to remove all the meat before the soup is finished in the microwave.

The traditional garnish of croûtons is easily prepared by toasting a few slices of bread under a preheated grill or in a toaster before spreading with a seasoned butter to complement the flavour of the soup.

The concept of the microwave as the quickest form of cooking since opening a packet is well proven in the preparation of quick snacks! Bought snacks and ready-prepared meals are, of course, quickly heated for serving and more and more commercially prepared products have microwave heating or cooking instructions on the packaging. However, the microwave enables you to prepare dishes from scratch in next to no time; several dishes here are ready to eat within 10–15min.

French Onion Soup

This soup is started on the hob to brown the onions and flour, and then transferred to the microwave to quickly finish cooking.

Serves 4 (opposite)

Soups & Snacks; top to bottom: Stuffed Baguette (page 12), French Onion Soup (above), Blue Cheese Toasts (page 12)

50g/2oz butter
225g/8oz onions, peeled and thinly sliced
2×15ml/tbsp flour
salt and pepper
bay leaf
750ml/1½pt boiling brown stock
4 slices french bread
40g/1½oz gruyère cheese, finely grated

1 Melt the butter in a saucepan on the hob, add the onions and cook for 10min until well browned.
2 Stir the flour into the onions and cook over a moderate heat until browned. Add salt and freshly ground pepper and a bay leaf.
3 Gradually stir the stock into the pan and heat until boiling, stirring constantly.
4 Pour the soup into a tureen that may be used in the microwave. Cover and cook for 10–12min.
5 Preheat the conventional grill. Sprinkle the bread with the grated gruyère cheese and heat under the grill until the cheese is melted and just starting to brown.
6 Remove the bay leaf, float the bread on top of the soup and serve immediately.

Chef's tip: Cook the onions over a moderate heat to brown. If you do not have homemade stock, use beef stock cubes for this recipe.

Serving suggestion: This soup is rich and filling. Serve before a light main course or a salad.

Freezer storage life: 6 months. Do not add the bread and cheese.

To defrost: Heat for 10–12min on 50%, then allow to stand for 10min.

To reheat: Heat for 8–10min, stirring twice. Add freshly toasted bread and cheese and serve.

Blue Cheese Toasts

Use your favourite blue cheese for this variation on Welsh Rarebit.

Serves 2 (see p10)

1 small onion, finely chopped
½ small green pepper, finely chopped
125g/4oz blue cheese, eg danish, stilton, roquefort, gorganzola etc, grated, sliced or crumbled
2 slices bread
paprika
salad to garnish

1 Preheat the conventional grill.
2 Place the chopped onion and pepper in a small covered microwave dish and cook for 2–3min, stirring once. Add the cheese.
3 Toast the bread under the grill on both sides, then top with the cheese and vegetables. Grill until the cheese has completely melted and is lightly browned.
4 Sprinkle the toasts with a little paprika. Cut into fingers and serve with a salad garnish.

Chef's tip: Most blue cheeses are best crumbled for cooking, either with the fingers or with a fork. Some are quite salty, so take care when seasoning. Do not freeze.

Stuffed Baguette

A quick supper snack that is simple to prepare and very filling.

Serves 2 (see p10)

1 small french stick
25g/1oz butter or margarine
1 large onion, finely sliced
½ red pepper, cut into strips
25g/1oz flour
250ml/10fl oz milk
200g/7oz can tuna fish, drained
125g/4oz button mushrooms, thickly sliced
few drops chilli sauce (optional)
salt and pepper

1 Preheat the oven to gas mark 6/200°C/400°F. Cut a slice from the top of the bread and hollow out the centre. Cut the loaf in two for easy serving. Heat the bread in the oven until required.
2 Melt the butter in a microwave dish for 1–2min, add the onion and pepper and cook for 3–4min, stirring once.
3 Add the flour to the vegetables and butter and mix well, then gradually stir in the milk. Heat for 4–6min or until the sauce has boiled and thickened, stirring every minute.
4 Add the tuna fish and mushrooms to the sauce and heat for a further 3–4min, then add the chilli sauce, if used, and seasonings to taste.
5 Fill the warmed bread stick and serve immediately.

Chef's tip: Make the bread removed from the stick into breadcrumbs and freeze for later use.

Serving suggestion: Serve with a small salad.

Freezer storage life: 3 months.

To defrost: Heat for 10–12min on 50%, then allow to stand for 10–15min.

To reheat: Heat for 20min in the conventional oven at gas mark 5/190°C/375°F. Reheating in the microwave will cause the bread to become soggy.

Chilled Lettuce & Pea Soup

A very delicate summer soup.

Serves 4–6

450g/1lb frozen petit pois
1 × 15ml/tbsp freshly chopped mint
salt
1 small lettuce, broken into leaves
750ml/1½pt boiling chicken stock
white pepper
125ml/5fl oz natural yogurt or single cream
chopped mint to garnish

1 Place the petits pois in a large microwave bowl, add the mint and a pinch of salt and cook, covered, for 5–6min, stirring once.
2 Wash the lettuce and shake dry. Tear the leaves and add them to the bowl. Pour the boiling stock over the lettuce, cover and leave for 3–4min until the lettuce has wilted.
3 Liquidise the soup in a food processor or blender and season to taste with salt and white pepper.
4 Allow the soup to cool then chill in the refrigerator for 3–4hr. Before serving, stir in the natural yogurt or cream and sprinkle with the chopped mint.

Chef's tip: If using a very crisp lettuce, such as webb's wonder or iceberg, it may be necessary to cook the lettuce for 2–3min in stage 2 to soften the stalks.

Serving suggestion: Delicious before a summer salad buffet.

Freezer storage life: 6 months. Do not add the yogurt or cream.

To defrost: Heat for 10–12min, then allow to stand for 10–15min before adding the yogurt or cream and whisking well.

Apple & Peanut Rarebits

Serves 1

1 small onion, finely chopped
2 slices bread
1 eating apple, cored and chopped
50–75g/2–3oz cheddar cheese, grated
½×5ml/tsp made mustard
peanut butter
sliced tomato to garnish

1 Preheat the conventional grill.
2 Place the onion in a small microwave dish and cook, covered, for 1–2min.
3 Add the apple, cheese and mustard to the onion and mix well.
4 Toast the bread on one side under the grill, then spread each slice with peanut butter. Top with the cheese mixture.
5 Grill the rarebits until the cheese has melted and is lightly browned. Serve garnished with sliced tomato.
Do not freeze.

Game Soup

For game soup, a stock is made by boiling the carcasses on the hob before finishing the soup in the microwave.

Serves 2

2 game bird carcasses
2litres/4pt water, approx
salt and pepper
225g/8oz yellow split peas
boiling water
2 large onions
2 stalks of celery
2 bay leaves

1 Place the carcasses, eg partridges, pheasants, pigeons, in a large saucepan with enough water to cover. Add salt and pepper, bring to the boil and simmer for 1–1½hr. Allow to cool.
2 While the carcasses are simmering, place the split peas in a bowl, cover with boiling water, then cover the dish and heat for 5min. Leave to stand for 1hr, then drain and rinse.
3 Pick the meat from the game carcasses and discard the bones and skin. Measure the stock and the meat together and make up to 1250ml/2½pt with water.
4 Place the onions and celery in a large bowl, cover and cook for 6–8min, stirring once. Add the drained split peas, the game stock and the bay leaves and a little extra salt and pepper. Cover and cook for 15min or until the soup is boiling rapidly.
5 Cook for a further 20–25min on 50%, or until the split peas are tender. Allow to cool slightly, remove the bay leaves, then liquidise and season to taste.

Serving suggestion: Serve with large chunks of fresh crusty bread for a substantial lunch or supper dish.

Freezer storage life: 3 months.

To defrost: Heat for 20–25min on 50%, then allow to stand for 15min.

To reheat: Heat for 12–15min on 100%, stirring once or twice.

Stuffed Mushrooms

In this recipe the mushrooms are stuffed, then grilled, whereas most stuffed mushrooms are deep-fat fried.

Serves 2 (see p39)

2 field mushrooms, about 15cm/6in diameter or
    4 large open mushrooms
2 or 4 slices bread, depending on the number
    of mushrooms
butter
75–125g/3–4oz pâté
25g/1oz cheddar cheese
25g/1oz breadcrumbs
parsley to garnish

1 Skin the mushrooms and cook on a plate for 5min, covered.
2 Preheat the grill and toast the bread on both sides. Butter the toast and place one mushroom on each slice.
3 Spread the pâté around the mushrooms, then sprinkle with the cheese and breadcrumbs. Toast until browned.
4 Garnish with parsley and serve immediately.
Do not freeze.

Pumpkin & Carrot Soup

A warming autumn soup, served with celery-flavoured croûtons.

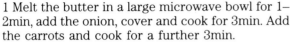

Serves 6 (opposite)

25g/1oz butter
1 large onion, finely sliced
225g/8oz carrots, peeled and sliced
450g/1lb prepared pumpkin flesh, diced
1×15ml/tbsp freshly chopped lovage or parsley
750ml/1½pt boiling vegetable stock
salt and pepper
40g/1½oz butter
celery salt
3 slices bread

1 Melt the butter in a large microwave bowl for 1–2min, add the onion, cover and cook for 3min. Add the carrots and cook for a further 3min.
2 Stir the pumpkin and lovage or parsley into the bowl and cook, covered, for 6–8min, stirring once.
3 Add the stock, with some salt and pepper to the vegetables. Cover and cook for 10–15min until the vegetables are tender. Stir once or twice during cooking.
4 Make the celery butter by beating the butter until soft, then adding celery salt and pepper to taste. Preheat the conventional grill.
5 Allow the soup to cool slightly, then liquidise in a blender or food processor until smooth. Check the seasoning.
6 Toast the bread and spread with the celery butter. Remove the crusts and cut into small triangles.
7 Serve the soup with the croûtons.

Chef's tip: Lovage is like many things – you've either got it or you haven't! Great thought should be given before planting as it is somewhat invasive and grows up to 2m/6ft high. A very peppery herb, it is ideal for soups but should be avoided when mixing fresh herbs as it could easily dominate the mixture.

Serving suggestion: As this soup is economical to make it is ideal for Hallowe'en and bonfire parties.

Freezer storage life: 12 months.

To defrost: Heat for 20–25min on 50%, then allow to stand for 10–15min.

To reheat: Heat for 8–10min on 100%, stirring once or twice.

left to right: Pumpkin & Carrot Soup (above), Pumpkin & Raisin Pie (page 82), Savoury Pumpkin Bread (page 90)

Mushroom Soup with Garlic Croûtons

This full-flavoured mushroom soup gives six helpings or four generous supper-sized portions.

Serves 4–6

50g/2oz butter
1 large onion, finely chopped
1 clove garlic, crushed
675g/1½lb mushrooms, chopped
1×15ml/tbsp freshly chopped sage or
  1×5ml/tsp dried sage
1 bay leaf
750ml/1½pt boiling vegetable or chicken stock
4×15ml/tbsp single cream

Garlic croûtons
50g/2oz butter
1×5ml/tsp onion, finely chopped
1–2 large cloves garlic, crushed
1×5ml/tsp freshly chopped parsley
4 slices bread
salt and freshly ground black pepper

1 Melt the butter in a large microwave bowl for 1–2min, add the onion and garlic, then cook for 3min, covered. Stir once during cooking.
2 Add the mushrooms, sage and bay leaf, cover and cook for 8–10min or until the mushrooms are softened. Stir once or twice.
3 Add the boiling stock, cover the bowl and cook for a further 10min.

4 While the soup is cooking, prepare a garlic butter for the croûtons. Beat the butter until soft, then add the 5ml/tsp onion, garlic and parsley. Season to taste with black pepper.
5 Preheat the conventional grill.
6 Remove the bay leaf and place the soup in a liquidiser or food processor and blend until smooth. Adjust the seasoning to taste.
7 Toast the bread on both sides under the grill before removing the crusts. Spread the toast with the garlic butter and cut into small triangles or shapes.
8 Stir the cream into the soup and serve with the croûtons scattered over the soup.

Chef's tip: Button mushrooms will give a pale, delicately coloured soup whereas open or field mushrooms produce a darker soup with a much stronger flavour.

Serving suggestion: This soup is fairly creamy so do not serve before a very rich main course.

Freezer storage life: 6 months. Freeze without the croûtons.

To defrost: Heat for 15–20min on 50%, then allow to stand for 10min.

To reheat: Heat for 8–10min on 100%, stirring once or twice. Add the croûtons, freshly cooked, and serve.

Borsch

The preparation time for this traditional Russian beetroot soup is cut considerably by using the pressure cooker and the microwave.

Serves 6

775g/1lb 12oz baby raw beetroot
250ml/10fl oz water
2 onions, finely sliced
2×15ml/tbsp lemon juice
5×15ml/tbsp dry sherry
1litre/2pt boiling beef stock
salt and pepper
soured cream to serve

1 Wash the beetroot and place them in a pressure cooker with the water. Cover and cook for 10min at 15lb/high pressure. Allow the pressure to reduce, then remove and peel the beetroot.
2 Place the onions, lemon juice and sherry in a large bowl. Cover and cook for 6min, or until the onions are soft, stirring once during cooking.
3 Blend together the peeled beetroot, onions and stock in a liquidiser or food processor, then season the soup to taste with salt and pepper.
4 Reheat the borsch for 3–4min. Garnish with soured cream before serving.

Chef's tip: Borsch is one of the few soups that is just as delicious hot or cold. Try serving chilled in the summer.

Freezer storage life: 6 months. Do not add the soured cream.

To defrost: Heat for 10–12min on 50%, then allow to stand for a further 10min.

To reheat: Heat for 10–12min on 100%, stirring once or twice. Add the soured cream and serve.

Bouillabaisse with Herb Bread

Serve this delicious soup from Marseilles as a starter or a light meal in itself.

Serves 6 (see p18)

Herb bread
1 french stick
125g/4oz butter
1×5ml/tsp onion, finely chopped
2–3×15ml/tbsp freshly chopped mixed herbs
salt and pepper

900g/2lb mixed fish, to include 6–8

varieties of white fish and shellfish but no smoked fish
2×15ml/tbsp olive oil
1 small onion, finely sliced
1 small leek, trimmed and sliced
2–3 cloves garlic, crushed
400g/14oz can chopped tomatoes
625ml/1¼pt boiling vegetable or fish stock
1×15ml/tbsp tomato paste
2×15ml/tbsp freshly chopped herbs, including sage
1 bay leaf

1 Preheat the conventional oven to gas mark 6/200°C/400°F.
2 Prepare the herb bread by slicing the french stick into 4cm/1½in pieces, not quite cutting through to the bottom of each slice. Heat the butter for 30–45sec to soften, if necessary, then beat in the herbs and chopped onion with a little salt and pepper. Spread the butter into the slits in the bread, then wrap the loaf in foil. Place in the preheated oven for 20min.
3 Prepare the fish by skinning any cutlets and fillets and cutting the fish into pieces of approx 2.5cm/1in. Cut huss into 1cm/½in slices. Monk fish should be taken off the bone after cooking, especially if using the tail.
4 Place the oil, onion, leek and garlic in a large covered microwave bowl and heat for 4min, stirring once. Add all the remaining ingredients, except any cooked shellfish, such as prawns, cockles and mussels. Cover and cook for 10min.
5 If using monk fish, remove the fish from the bowl, take the flesh from the bone and return it to the bouillabaisse. Add the shellfish and cook for a further 3–4min.
6 Remove the bay leaf, season to taste and serve with the herb bread.

Chef's tip: Find a friendly fishmonger! Most are happy to help, if you explain what you are making.
   The secret of a good herb or garlic bread is to add a little chopped onion to the butter as it prevents any bitter flavour.

Freezer storage life: Up to 6 months for the herb bread, 1 month for the bouillabaisse. Do not freeze the soup if it is made with previously frozen shellfish.

To defrost: Heat the soup for 12–15min on 50%, then allow to stand for 10min.

To reheat: Reheat the bread from frozen in a preheated oven at gas mark 6/200°C/400°F for 20min. Heat the bouillabaisse for 10–12min in the microwave, at 100%, stirring once or twice.

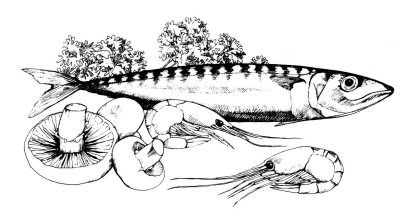

Starters & Hors d'Oeuvres

A starter is the overture to a meal – it sets the scene for what is to come, and it is important, therefore, that it is colourful, interesting and not too filling.

If a rich main course is to be served, choose a starter that is light and a good contrast to what is to follow. Avoid serving a meaty starter before a red meat main course.

Garlic lovers often say that they would like a whole meal of starters as many do use garlic. However, remember it is a very strong flavour, and do not serve a strongly garlic starter before a delicately flavoured main course.

Many of the soups in the previous chapter may also be used to start a meal. See also Greek Chicken Salad (p66), Mushroom & French Bean Salad (p105), Curried Petits Choux with Coriander Sauce (p106) and Pâté du Maison (p114).

Seafood Tartlets

Delicious tartlets of shellfish in a wine sauce which may be served as a starter or a light supper dish.

Serves 4 (opposite)

Pastry
175g/6oz flour
75g/3oz butter
1 egg yolk
water to mix

Bouillabaise with Herb Bread (page 17), Seafood Tartlets (above)

Filling
4 large scallops, sliced
75ml/3fl oz dry white wine
1×15ml/tbsp freshly chopped dill
25g/1oz butter
15g/½oz flour
75ml/3fl oz milk
4×15ml tbsp single cream
salt and pepper
125g/4oz peeled prawns
125g/4oz cockles
1×15ml/tbsp freshly chopped chives

Salad
watercress
2 oranges, cut into segments with
    peel and pith removed
1 large avocado, peeled and sliced
lemon juice

1 Preheat the conventional oven to gas mark 5/ 190°C/375°F. Lightly grease 4 deep individual quiche tins, approx 10cm/4in in diameter.
2 Place the flour in a large bowl and rub in the butter until the mixture resembles fine breadcrumbs. Add the egg yolk and sufficient water to mix to a stiff dough.
3 Knead the pastry gently on a lightly floured board, then divide into four and roll out to line the quiche tins. Line with paper and baking beans and bake blind in the preheated oven for 15–20min. Remove the paper and beans and cook for a further 5min.
4 While the pastry cases are cooking, poach the scallops in a covered microwave dish with the wine and the chopped dill for 3–4min until just tender – do not overcook. Put to one side.
5 Melt the butter for 1min in a jug or bowl, then add the flour and beat well. Remove the scallops from the wine and beat the wine and the milk into the mixture. Heat for 2–3min or until boiling and

thickened, stirring every minute. Season to taste and add the cream.

6 Mix the prawns and the cockles with the scallops and add the chopped chives. Add to the sauce and heat for 3–4min on 70%.

7 Place the fish filling in the warm pastry cases and serve with a small salad of watercress, orange segments and sliced avocado, sprinkled with lemon juice.

Chef's tip: Test scallops during cooking with a sharp knife. When cooked they should offer no resistance to the knife. Do not overcook or they will become rubbery.

Serving suggestion: Serve as a starter before a light main course, or as a lunch or supper dish.

Freezer storage life: 3 months. Do not freeze if using previously frozen shellfish.

To defrost: Heat the tartlets for 12–15min on 30%, then allow to stand for 20min.

To reheat: Heat for 20min in the conventional oven at gas mark 4/180°C/350°F. Microwave reheating will cause the pastry to become soggy.

Humus

Homemade humus is more economical than that bought from a delicatessen, and much less oily.

Serves 4–6

225g/8oz chick peas
salt
100ml/4fl oz olive oil
175g/6oz tahini, approx
2–3 cloves garlic, crushed
1 lemon, grated rind and juice
freshly ground black pepper
paprika, lemon or olives to garnish
pitta bread to serve

1 Place the chick peas in a large microwave dish and cover with boiling water. Cover the dish and heat for 5min, then allow the chick peas to stand for 1hr before draining and rinsing.

2 For a smooth textured humus, place the chick peas in a saucepan of water with a pinch of salt. Bring to the boil, then cover and simmer for 45min or until the peas are soft. For a more textured humus, place the chick peas in a microwave dish and cover with fresh boiling water. Cover the dish

and cook for 10min on 100%, then a further 15–20min on 50%.

3 Drain the chick peas, reserving the cooking water, and place the peas in a liquidiser or food processor with the olive oil, tahini, garlic, lemon rind and juice. Process to a thick purée, adding a little of the cooking water if required.

4 Season the humus to taste with salt and freshly ground black pepper then spoon into a serving dish and chill in the refrigerator for at least 2hr.

5 Garnish with paprika, lemon butterflies or olives before serving with pitta bread fingers. The bread may be heated under a hot grill or in the microwave before serving, allowing 45sec for 4 pittas.

Chef's tip: Using the cooking water from the chick peas to blend the humus instead of extra oil makes the dish far less oily than some ready prepared humus.

Freezer storage life: 6 months.

To defrost: Heat for 10min on 50%, then allow to stand for 10min. Beat well.

Pear & Whitebait Salad

This salad, which combines devilled whitebait with pears and grapefruit, makes a welcome change from deep-fried whitebait.

Serves 8 (see p83)

450g/1lb frozen whitebait
3×15ml/tbsp flour
2 firm comice pears
lemon juice
1 ripe avocado
oil for frying
salt and cayenne
4 segments grapefruit (fresh or canned)
fresh shredded spinach to serve
lemon or lime wedges to garnish

1 Place the whitebait on a large plate, heat for 6–8min on 30%, then allow to stand for 10min.

2 Sprinkle the flour on the whitebait.

3 Score the skins of the comice pears and cook on 70% for 6–8min until just soft. Allow to cool, then peel, core, dice and toss in lemon juice. Peel the avocado and remove the stone. Dice the avocado and toss in the lemon juice.

4 Heat some oil in a large frying pan, add the whitebait a few at a time and cook for 2–3min until crisp. Drain on kitchen paper, sprinkle lightly with salt and cayenne and allow to cool.

5 Mix together the whitebait, pears and avocado. Dice the grapefruit segments and add to the whitebait. Season to taste and chill for 1–2hr.
6 Serve on a bed of shredded spinach; garnish with lemon or lime wedges.

Chef's tip: Do not rush the preparation of this salad by cooking too many whitebait at a time. They will stay a better shape if only a few are cooked at once.

Serving suggestion: This salad travels well in an ice-box and is good for special picnics.
Do not freeze.

Mackerel Pâté

Serves 4–6

Pâté
225g/8oz smoked mackerel fillets
125g/4oz butter
1×5ml/tsp horseradish mustard or sauce
1 lemon, grated rind
freshly ground black pepper
2×15ml/tbsp soured or single cream

Garnish
freshly chopped parsley and grated lemon rind

For serving
4–6 slices medium cut bread, crusts removed

1 Place the mackerel fillets in a covered microwave dish and cook for 3–4min. Allow to cool for 5min, skin and flake the fish, and remove any bones.
2 While the fish is cooling, heat the butter in a small dish for 3min or until melted. Allow to cool until required.
3 Place the flaked mackerel, butter and horseradish in a liquidiser or food processor and blend until smooth. Add the grated lemon rind and season to taste with black pepper, then stir in the cream.
4 Spoon the pâté into a serving dish and chill in the refrigerator for 2–3hr.
5 To serve, preheat the conventional grill, then toast the bread on both sides. Using a very sharp bread knife, carefully cut horizontally through the slices. Toast the cut surfaces of the bread, then cut it into fingers.
6 Mix together some chopped parsley and grated lemon rind and sprinkle over the pâté before serving with the melba toasts.

Chef's tip: If you buy boil-in-the-bag mackerel fillets they may be cooked from frozen. Slit the bag and place on a plate.

Melba toast is very simple to make but must be watched closely when grilling the cut surface of the bread, as it tends to cook very quickly. The toast may be prepared in advance and stored in an air-tight tin.

Serving suggestion: This is a rich pâté and is best served before a not-too-rich main course, such as Oven Baked Lamb with Shrewsbury Sauce (p56) or Chicken with Peaches & Almonds (p57).

Freezer storage life: 2 months.

To defrost: Defrost overnight in the refrigerator to prevent the cream from separating.

Egg Mousse with Prawns

A light starter that will complement a rich main course well.

Serves 6 (see p23)

125ml/5fl oz milk
2 peppercorns
small piece carrot
small piece onion
small piece celery
6 eggs
15g/½oz butter
15g/½oz flour
salt and pepper
125ml/5fl oz mayonnaise
3×15ml/tbsp water
1×15ml/tbsp powdered gelatine
2 egg whites
125g/4oz peeled prawns
cress and paprika to garnish

1 Pour the milk into a bowl and add the peppercorns, carrot, onion and celery. Heat for 1–2min, then cover and allow to stand for 10min. Strain and reserve the milk.
2 Place the eggs in a pan of cold water, bring to the boil and cook for 8–10min on the hob. Drain the eggs immediately, crack the shells then stand in cold water until cooled.
3 Melt the butter in a bowl for 1min then add the flour and mix well. Gradually stir in the milk. Heat for 2–3min or until boiling and thickened, stirring every minute. Season lightly to taste with salt and pepper. Cover the sauce with greaseproof paper to prevent a skin from forming.
4 Shell the eggs and remove the yolks from the whites. Press the yolks through a nylon sieve and finely chop the whites. Place in a mixing bowl.
5 Combine the eggs with the sauce and mayonnaise.

6 Heat the water in a small bowl or cup for 1min, then sprinkle with the gelatine and stir well. Heat for a further 15–20sec until the gelatine is completely dissolved, then stir into the egg mixture. Season the mousse to taste.

7 Allow the mousse to stand for 10–15min.

8 Whisk the egg whites until stiff, then fold into the mousse. Pour into a 20cm/8in microwave ring mould. Refrigerate until set.

9 Turn the mousse out onto a serving plate and fill the centre with prawns. Decorate the edge of the plate with cress and sprinkle the mousse with a little paprika.

Chef's tip: Do not overcook the eggs as it makes them very difficult to peel and causes black lines around the yolks.

Serving suggestion: Serve with melba toast (p21) or biscuits as a starter. The mousse may also be served as part of a cold buffet with smoked or dressed salmon.
Do not freeze.

Avocados with Raspberry Purée

Visually stunning, an unusual combination of fruits for a starter.

Serves 4 (opposite)

225g/8oz raspberries
caster sugar to taste
2 avocados
lemon juice

1 Place the raspberries in a small covered dish and cook for 3–4min or until soft, stirring once during cooking. Add sugar to sweeten, if necessary, then rub the fruit through a nylon sieve to remove the pips. Chill.

2 Halve the avocados and remove the stones. Brush with lemon juice to prevent browning.

3 Serve either by filling the avocados with the raspberry purée, or peel and slice the avocados and serve the sauce with the slices.

Chef's tip: It is not always possible to buy avocados at the right point of ripeness on the day that they are required. It is often best to shop for them two or three days before needed, then ripen them in the airing cupboard.

Serving suggestion: This starter is easy to prepare and the purée can be made well in advance.
Do not freeze.

Ham & Asparagus Crêpes

Serves 6

1 egg, beaten
250ml/10fl oz milk
125g/4oz flour
salt
oil for frying
340g/12oz can asparagus spears
25g/1oz butter or margarine
25g/1oz flour
250ml/10fl oz milk
pepper
12 thin slices of ham
50g/2oz gruyère cheese, finely grated
parsley to garnish

1 Place the egg and milk in a liquidiser or food processor and whisk together. Add the flour and a pinch of salt and blend well. Alternatively, beat the flour and egg and gradually whisk in the milk.

2 Heat a little oil in an omelette or small frying pan. Use the batter to make 12 thin pancakes or crêpes, adding extra oil as required. Place each crêpe on kitchen paper as they are cooked to avoid them sticking together.

3 Drain the asparagus spears and chop.

4 Melt the butter in a microwave jug or bowl for 1–2min, add the flour and mix well. Gradually add the milk, then heat the sauce for 4–5min or until boiling and thickened, stirring every minute.

5 Season the sauce to taste with salt and pepper, then add the chopped asparagus.

6 Place a slice of ham on each crêpe, then a little of the asparagus sauce. Roll the crêpes, then place in a serving dish suitable for the microwave and for the grill.

7 Cover the dish and heat for 6min on 70%. While the crêpes are in the microwave preheat the grill.

8 Scatter the grated cheese over the crêpes and grill until melted and slightly browned.

9 Garnish with parsley and serve.

Chef's tip: The crêpes may be prepared in advance to the end of stage 6, then reheated for 8min in stage 7, then browned under the grill.

Freezer storage life: 3 months.

To defrost: Heat for 8–10min on 30%, then allow to stand for 20min at room temperature.

To reheat: Heat for 6–8min on 70%.

Starters; top to bottom: Avocado with Raspberry Purée (above), Nut and Cream Cheese Peppers (page 25), Egg Mousse with Prawns (page 21)

Choux Buns Provençale

Choux buns, served cold with a fish filling and yogurt sauce, perfectly complement a rich meat entrée. See Curried Petits Choux with Coriander Sauce (p106) for an alternative filling.

Serves 4

Choux Buns
40g/1½oz butter
100ml/4fl oz water
6×level 15ml/tbsp flour, sieved
1 egg + 1 yolk, beaten together

Filling
25g/1oz butter
1 small onion, finely chopped
1 clove garlic, crushed
225g/8oz cod fillet, skinned
2×15ml/tbsp freshly chopped parsley
200g/7oz can chopped tomatoes

Sauce
6×15ml/tbsp natural yogurt
grated rind 1 lemon
1–2×15ml/tbsp freshly chopped parsley
salt and pepper
cress to garnish

1 Preheat the oven to gas mark 7/210°C/425°F. Lightly grease a large baking sheet.
2 Place the butter and water in a saucepan and heat on the hob until the butter is melted. Bring to a fast boil, then shoot the sieved flour into the pan and beat well, off the heat. The mixture should form a ball and come away from the sides of the pan.
3 Allow the pastry to cool slightly, then gradually beat in the eggs to give a piping consistency. Place the pastry on the baking sheet in 12 small spoonfuls and bake in the preheated oven for 20min.
4 Make a small slit in each bun with a sharp knife, then return them to the oven. Reduce the temperature to gas mark 5/190°C/375°F and bake for a further 10–15min. Allow to cool on a wire rack.
5 To make the filling, melt the butter in a microwave dish for 1–2min, add the onion and garlic, cover and cook for 2–3min. Add the cod, cover and cook for a further 3min.
6 Remove the cod from the dish and set to one side.
7 Add the tomatoes and parsley to the onion and cook, uncovered, for 6–8min, or until reduced and thickened.
8 While the sauce is cooking, flake the fish, removing any bones. Return the fish to the sauce

and season with salt and pepper. Allow to cool completely, then chill in the refrigerator for 1–2hr.
9 Prepare the sauce by stirring the lemon rind and chopped parsley into the yogurt, then season to taste with salt and pepper.
10 Fill each of the choux buns with a little of the cod provençale and place three buns on each plate. Garnish the plates with a little cress.
11 Pour the yogurt sauce over the buns immediately before serving.

Chef's tip: Prepare the cod filling well in advance, allowing at least 2hr for cooling and chilling. The choux buns may be made the day before they are required and stored in an air-tight tin.

Freezer storage life: 3 months. Freeze the buns and the cod sauce separately. Do not freeze the yogurt sauce.

To defrost: Allow 10–12min at 50% with a 10min standing period for the cod provençale, and 5–8min at 50% with a 15min standing period for the choux buns.

Spiced Bean Dip

Served warm with tortilla chips this dip makes a perfect start to a Mexican meal.

Serves 4–6

225g/8oz red kidney beans
1 small onion, chopped
salt
chilli sauce
125ml/5fl oz soured cream
tortilla chips for serving

1 Place the kidney beans in a large microwave dish and cover with boiling water. Cover the dish and heat for 5min, then allow the beans to stand for 1hr. Drain and rinse the beans.
2 Place the beans in a saucepan of water with a pinch of salt. Bring to the boil for 10min, then cover and simmer for a further 30min or until the beans are soft. Drain, reserving the cooking liquid.
3 Place the cooked beans in a blender or food processor with the onion and process until smooth, adding a little cooking liquid as required.
4 Season the purée with salt and chilli sauce.
5 Stir the soured cream into the dip, then spoon into a serving dish.
6 If serving immediately, reheat in the microwave for 1min, if necessary. If preparing the dip in advance, reheat for 3–4min before serving, stirring once. Serve with tortilla chips.

Chef's tip: Don't make the dip too spicy as good tortilla chips will be well seasoned.

Freezer storage life: 6 months. Do not add the soured cream.

To defrost: Heat for 10min on 50%, then allow to stand for 10min.

To reheat: Heat for 3–4min on 100%, stir in the soured cream and heat for a further 1min.

Nut & Cream Cheese Peppers

A slice of green and a slice of red pepper makes a colourful starter.

Serves 4 (see p23)

3×15ml/tbsp olive oil
225g/8oz mixed nuts, eg shelled peanuts, almonds, cashews, hazelnuts, etc
salt
cayenne pepper
175g/6oz cream cheese
1 clove garlic, crushed
freshly ground black pepper
1 medium red pepper
1 medium green pepper
toast fingers to serve

1 Heat the oil on a microwave plastic plate for 3min, then add the nuts and toss well. Cook for 4–5min until browned, then remove the nuts using a slotted spoon and drain on kitchen paper.
2 Place the nuts in a dish or on greaseproof paper and sprinkle with salt and cayenne pepper. Toss from time to time until the nuts are cool. Roughly chop the nuts when cold.
3 Beat the cream cheese until smooth, then add the crushed garlic and the nuts. Season to taste with black pepper.
4 Cut the tops from the peppers and reserve. Cut away and discard the core and seeds. Wash and dry the peppers.
5 Fill the peppers with the nut cheese, pressing down firmly with the back of a teaspoon. Replace the lids on the peppers.
6 Chill for 2–3hr to set the filling.
7 To serve, cut the peppers into slices and serve 1 red and 1 green slice per person, with freshly cooked toast fingers.

Freezer storage life: 3 months for the nut filling. Do not freeze the peppers.

To defrost: Heat for 10min on 30%, then allow to stand for 15min. Beat well, then use to fill the peppers. Chill before serving as above.

Smoked Trout & Parma Ham Mousse

The flavours of the trout and parma ham combine beautifully in this rich starter, served with balls of melon.

Serves 8

250ml/10fl oz milk
6 peppercorns
1 blade mace
small piece celery
small piece carrot
small piece onion
25g/1oz butter or margarine
25g/1oz flour
1×15ml/tbsp freshly chopped dill (optional)
salt and white pepper to taste
125g/4oz parma ham
450g/1lb smoked trout
250ml/10fl oz double cream
3×15ml/tbsp water
1 heaped 15ml/tbsp gelatine, or 1 sachet
2 egg whites
melon balls and toast fingers to serve

1 Place the milk in a large jug with the peppercorns, mace, celery, carrot and onion. Heat for 4min, then cover the jug and allow to stand for 10min to allow the seasonings to flavour the milk. Strain the milk and discard the flavourings.
2 Melt the butter in a jug or bowl for 1–2min, add the flour and stir well. Gradually add the flavoured milk. Cook for 2–3min or until boiling and thickened, stirring every minute. Add the dill, if used, and season to taste with salt and pepper.
3 Prepare a 23–25cm/9–10in ring mould. If using a plastic microwave mould, lightly oil it and line the base with a circle of non-stick baking parchment. Rinse a metal mould under the cold water tap.
4 Line the mould with alternate slices of parma ham and smoked trout, slightly overlapping each piece.
5 Place the sauce in a liquidiser or blender with the remaining trout and ham. Process until the trout and ham are finely chopped and well blended with the sauce.
6 Whisk the cream until thick but still soft and fold into the sauce. Season to taste with salt and white pepper.
7 Heat the water in a small bowl for 1min, sprinkle with the gelatine and stir well. Heat for 15sec to dissolve the gelatine but do not allow the liquid to boil. Cool slightly, then stir into the trout cream.
8 Whisk the egg whites until stiff, then fold into the trout cream.
9 Spoon the mixture into the lined ring mould. Fold the ends of the trout and ham over the filling,

then chill for 2–3hr until set.

10 Ease the set mousse away from the sides of the dish, then turn out onto a serving plate. Fill the centre of the ring mould with melon balls, then chill until required.

11 Just before serving, preheat the grill and toast one slice of bread per person on each side. Remove the crusts and cut into fingers.

12 Serve the mousse sliced with a few balls of melon and the toast fingers.

Chef's tip: To slice the trout you will need a very sharp thin bladed knife. If buying the trout from a delicatessen, ask the assistant to remove 5 or 6 thin slices from your portion to line the mould. Alternatively, line the ring mould with parma ham and use all the trout to make the mousse.

Serving suggestion: This is a rich starter, ideal for serving before a salad in the summer. If you have a black serving plate, the effect will be very sophisticated.

Do not freeze.

Chilli Prawn Tacos

A quick Mexican dish, prepared at the drop of a sombrero, which may be served as a starter or as a snack.

Serves 4 (opposite)

1 avocado, ripe but firm
1×15ml/tbsp lemon juice
125g/4oz cream cheese
8 taco shells
1 onion, finely sliced
225g/8oz peeled prawns
bottled chilli, or chilli and garlic sauce,
    to taste
lettuce to serve

1 Preheat the oven to gas mark 5/190°C/375°F.

2 Peel the avocado and remove the stone. Place in a liquidiser or blender with the lemon juice and cream cheese and process until smooth.

3 Place the taco shells, open edge downwards, on a baking sheet in the preheated oven for 10min.

4 Place the onion in a covered dish and cook for 2–3min until soft. Add the prawns and cook for 2–3min until piping hot. Add the chilli sauce to taste.

5 Spoon a little of the avocado purée into each taco shell, then top with prawns.

6 Serve immediately on a bed of lettuce.

Serving suggestion: These may be served before any main course, or as a supper dish.

Do not freeze.

Beef Tostadas

A traditional Mexican dish, tostadas make a good starter and you can experiment with your own toppings. This is a traditional minced beef recipe.

Serves 4 (opposite)

2×15ml/tbsp oil
1 onion, finely sliced
½×5ml/tsp chilli powder
450g/1lb minced beef
2×15ml/tbsp tomato paste
salt and pepper
8 tostadas
125g/4oz cheddar cheese, grated
shredded lettuce, chopped tomatoes and black
    olives to garnish

1 Preheat the conventional oven to gas mark 5/ 190°C/375°F.

2 Heat the oil in a microwave casserole dish for 2min, add the onion and chilli powder and cook, covered, for 2–3min. Add the minced beef and cook for 4min, stirring once.

3 Stir the tomato paste into the beef with a little salt and pepper and cook on 50% for 15min.

4 Place the tostadas in the preheated oven and heat for 10min or as directed.

5 Check the seasoning of the minced beef.

6 To serve, pile the beef onto the tostadas then garnish with the shredded lettuce, chopped tomatoes and olives.

Chef's tip: Tostadas are flat, crispy cereal shells. They are available in most large supermarkets and delicatessens.

Serving suggestion: Serve as part of a Mexican meal; see also Spiced Bean Dip (p24), Bean & Raisins Enchiladas (p28) and Chilli Prawn Tacos (above).

Freezer storage life: 3 months for beef topping. Do not freeze the tostadas.

To defrost: Heat for 5–8min on 50%, then allow to stand for 10min.

To reheat: Heat the beef for 5–6min on 100%, stirring once or twice.

left to right: Beef Tostadas (above), Bean & Raisin Enchiladas (page 28), Chilli Prawn Tacos (above)

Lunch & Supper Dishes

Lunch and supper dishes should be quick to prepare and not too filling. The recipes in this chapter only require a little salad to garnish, and most can be prepared and cooked in 30–40min.

Bean & Raisin Enchiladas

Enchiladas are Mexican pancakes, made using corn tortillas. Traditionally filled with minced beef, this bean and raisin stuffing makes a delicious Mexican-style vegetarian dish.

Serves 4 (see p27)

225g/8oz broad beans, fresh or frozen
25g/1oz butter
1 onion, finely chopped
1 clove garlic, crushed
½ × 5ml/tsp chilli powder
125g/4oz cooked rice
25g/1oz raisins
salt and pepper
8 tortilla pancakes
oil for frying
400g/14oz can chopped tomatoes
50–75g/2–3oz cheddar cheese, grated

1 Preheat the oven to gas mark 5/190°C/375°F.
2 Place the broad beans in a covered microwave dish with 2–3 x 15ml/tbsp water. Cook for 4–5min, stirring once.
3 Melt the butter in a bowl for 1–2min, add the onion, garlic and chilli powder and cook, covered, for 2–3min.
4 Drain the broad beans and add to the onion with the rice and raisins. Season to taste with salt and pepper.
5 Heat 1cm/½in oil in a frying pan. Fry the tortillas in the hot oil for a few seconds only on each side. Drain on kitchen paper.
6 Spoon a little of the bean mixture into each tortilla, roll up and place in an ovenproof serving dish. Place any remaining filling around the tortillas.
7 Pour the tomatoes over and finish with the grated cheese. Bake in the preheated oven for 30–40min until the cheese is melted and browned.

Chef's tip: Fry the tortillas for just a few seconds on either side; overcooking will cause them to split when rolled.

Serving suggestion: Serve with a salad including avocado. Natural yogurt will soften the heat of the chilli.

Freezer storage life: 6 months.

To defrost: Heat for 12–15min on 50%, then allow to stand for 10–15min.

To reheat: Heat for 10–12min on 70%.

Spiced Peanut & Sweetcorn Pancakes

These savoury pancakes make a good vegetarian dish.

Serves 4 (see p31)

Batter
250ml/10fl oz milk or milk and water
1 egg, beaten
125g/4oz flour
salt and pepper
oil for frying

Sauce
1 onion, finely chopped
25g/1oz margarine or butter
pinch of chilli powder
25g/1oz flour
340g/12oz can sweetcorn kernels
125g/4oz peanut kernels
250ml/10fl oz milk (approx)
75g/3oz cheddar or gruyère cheese, grated

1 Prepare the pancake batter by placing the milk and egg in a liquidiser or processor and blending together before adding the flour and seasonings and processing until smooth. Alternatively, blend the flour, egg and seasonings in a bowl and gradually beat in the milk.
2 Heat a little oil in an omelette pan and use the batter to make 12 pancakes, adding extra oil to the pan as required.
3 To make the sauce, place the onion in a small covered dish and cook in the microwave for 2–3min on 100%.
4 Place the margarine or butter in a large jug or bowl with the chilli powder and heat for 1–2min. Stir in the flour.
5 Strain any liquid from the sweetcorn and make up to 250ml/10fl oz with milk. Gradually add the liquid to the butter and flour, stirring well.
6 Cook the sauce for 4–5min or until boiling and thickened, stirring every minute. Add 50g/2oz of the cheese and season to taste with salt and pepper.
7 Stir the onion, sweetcorn and peanuts into the sauce and use the mixture to fill the pancakes, placing them in a large microwave-to-oven serving dish.
8 Cover the dish and heat for 5–6min on 70%. Meanwhile, preheat the grill.
9 Sprinkle the remaining cheese over the pancakes and brown under the grill.

Chef's tip: When cooking pancakes that are to be filled, layer the pancakes as they are cooked between pieces of kitchen paper. This prevents them from sticking to each other.

Serving suggestion: Serve with green vegetables such as broccoli or calabrese, or a crisp green or lettuce salad. Wholewheat bread and butter may also be served with the pancakes if required.

Freezer storage life: 3 months.

To defrost: Heat for 10–12min on 30%, then allow to stand for 15–20min.

To reheat: Heat for 8–10min on 70%.

Mixed Grain Risotto

Commercially prepared mixtures of rice and other grains, such as wheat, rye and sesame seeds, are now available in health food shops and supermarkets; or make your own by mixing any small grains with at least 25 per cent rice.

Serves 4

1 cooked chicken carcase
water to cover
225g/8oz mixed rice and grains
1 large onion, finely sliced
1 clove garlic, crushed
1 red pepper, seeded and cut into strips
125g/4oz frozen peas
1×15ml/tbsp lemon juice
1×15ml/tbsp olive oil
1×15ml/tbsp freshly chopped herbs
salt and pepper
chopped parsley to garnish

1 Place the chicken carcase in a saucepan and cover with water. Simmer for 45–60min on the hob until all the meat on the carcase can be easily removed and the stock is well reduced.
2 Remove the chicken from the stock and reserve 500ml/1pt of the liquid.
3 Place the mixed rice and grains in a large bowl, add the measured stock, cover and cook in the microwave for 25–30min, or until the water is absorbed.
4 While the grains are cooking, remove the meat from the chicken and discard the bones.
5 Allow the grains to stand, covered. Cook the onion and garlic in a large shallow dish, covered, for 2–3min, then add the pepper and the peas and cook for a further 4–5min.
6 Prepare the dressing by shaking together the lemon juice, oil and herbs in a screw-top jar.
7 Stir the grains and the chicken into the dish with the dressing. Heat, uncovered, for 4–5min, or until piping hot.
8 Season to taste and serve, garnished with chopped parsley.

Variation: This risotto may also be made using a yellow pepper with 225g/8oz frozen broad beans. Allow 6–8min to cook the vegetables in stage 4.

Freezer storage life: 3 months.

To defrost: Heat for 15min on 50%, then allow to stand for 10min.

To reheat: Heat for 5–6min on 100%, stirring once.

Wholewheat Salami & Mushroom Pizza

Homemade pizzas give the opportunity to experiment with a wide variety of delicious toppings. Preparing a yeast dough for the base in the microwave before baking the pizza in the conventional oven speeds the preparation time.

Serves 5–6 (opposite)

Base
175g/6oz wholewheat flour
50g/2oz strong plain flour
½×5ml/tsp salt
3×15ml/tbsp oil
1 egg, beaten
15g/½oz fresh yeast or
　1 sachet easy-blend dried yeast
125ml/5fl oz milk, approx

Topping
1 large onion, finely chopped
1 clove garlic, crushed
400g/14oz can chopped tomatoes
1×15ml/tbsp tomato paste
225g/8oz mushrooms, sliced
175g/6oz small danish salami, finely sliced
salt and freshly ground black pepper
1×15ml/tbsp freshly chopped marjoram
oil
125g/4oz mozzarella cheese, drained and grated
50g/2oz can anchovies
olives

1 Mix together the flours and the salt and add the dried yeast, if used. Make a well in the centre and add the oil and egg.
2 Heat the milk for 20–30sec until tepid. Cream the fresh yeast, if used, with a little of the warm milk and add to the flour. Mix the flours with sufficient of the tepid milk to make a workable dough. Turn onto a floured board and knead until smooth.
3 Place the dough in a covered bowl and heat for 15sec, then allow to stand for 10min. Repeat 3–4 times until the dough is well risen and doubled in size.
4 Knock back lightly and roll out to a circle approx 30cm/12in in diameter. Place on a greased baking sheet and cover with a plastic bag or cooking film and leave in a warm place for approx 15min.
5 Preheat the conventional oven to gas mark 6/200°C/400°F while preparing the pizza topping. Place the onion and garlic in a bowl, cover and cook in the microwave for 4min, stirring once. Add the tomatoes, tomato paste, mushrooms and

seasonings and stir well. Cook for 10min, uncovered, then adjust the seasoning to taste.
6 Brush the risen pizza dough with a little oil, then arrange half the salami slices on the dough. Spoon the tomato mixture over the dough and decorate with the remaining salami.
7 Place the mozzarella on the pizza and decorate with the drained anchovies and a few olives.
8 Bake the pizza in the preheated oven for 20–25min, then serve immediately.

Chef's tip: Canned anchovies are very salty and may be soaked in milk before use to remove some of the excess salt.

Serving suggestion: Serve with sliced tomatoes or a mixed side salad, topped with freshly chopped herbs and mayonnaise or blue cheese dressing.

Freezer storage life: 3 months.

To defrost: Heat for 10min on 50%, then allow to stand for 15–20min.

To reheat: Heat for 8–10min on 70%, uncovered. Slices of pizza may be reheated on a browning dish, which will prevent the bread base from becoming soggy.

Curried Lentil Soufflé

The flavour of curry is not often found in a soufflé but in this substantial supper dish the combination works well.

Serves 3 (opposite)

125g/4oz orange lentils
1–2×5ml/tsp curry powder
250ml/10fl oz boiling chicken or
　vegetable stock
25g/1oz butter or margarine
25g/1oz flour
125ml/5fl oz milk
3 eggs, separated
salt and pepper
pinch dry mustard powder

1 Place the lentils, curry powder and stock in a large covered dish and cook for 10–12min on

top to bottom: Curried Lentil Soufflé (above), Spiced Peanut & Sweetcorn Pancakes (page 28), Wholewheat Salami & Mushroom Pizza (above)

100% until thick. Beat well, then allow the lentils to cool.

2 Preheat the conventional oven to gas mark 4/ 180°C/350°F and lightly grease a 15cm/6in soufflé dish.

3 Melt the butter or margarine in a large bowl for 1–2min, then whisk in the flour. Gradually add the milk, whisking continuously, then heat for 2–3min until very thick, stirring every minute.

4 Add the egg yolks and the lentil purée to the sauce, then add a pinch of mustard and season to taste with salt and pepper.

5 Whisk the egg whites until stiff, then fold them into the lentil paste. Pour the mixture into the prepared dish.

6 Bake in the preheated oven for 30–35min until well risen and set. Serve immediately.

Chef's tip: Orange lentils are the only pulse vegetable that does not require soaking before cooking. This makes them ideal for a quick supper dish, such as this soufflé.

Serving suggestion: Serve with a salad of sliced tomatoes with a little raw onion and freshly chopped coriander.
Do not freeze.

Macaroni & Vegetable Cheese

Serves 4

225g/8oz macaroni
1×15ml/tbsp oil
salt and pepper
75g/3oz butter or margarine
1 large onion, finely sliced
1 clove garlic, crushed
225g/8oz prepared mixed vegetables, sliced
  or diced
50g/2oz flour
375ml/15fl oz milk
125g/4oz cheddar cheese, grated
3×15ml/tbsp single cream

1 Bring a large pan of water to the boil on the hob, then add the macaroni with the oil and a pinch of salt. Cook for 10min or as directed.

2 Melt 25g/1oz butter or margarine in a large microwave serving dish, suitable for use under the grill, for 1–2min. Add the onion and garlic and cook for 2–3min. Add the prepared vegetables and cook for a further 6–8min until the vegetables are tender.

3 Drain the pasta and add to the vegetables. Season with salt and pepper.

4 Melt the remaining butter or margarine in a microwave bowl for 2–3min, add the flour and stir well. Gradually add the milk. Cook for 6–7min, or until boiling and thickened, stirring every minute. Add most of the cheese and the cream, then season the sauce to taste.

5 Preheat the conventional grill.

6 Pour the sauce into the serving dish and mix well with the macaroni and vegetables. Sprinkle the remaining cheese over the dish.

7 Brown the top of the vegetables under the grill.

Serving suggestion: Serve with a coleslaw salad and crusty bread.

Freezer storage life: 4 months.

To defrost: Heat for 15–18min on 50%, then allow to stand for 10min.

To reheat: Heat for 10–12min at 70%.

Pepper & Roquefort Quichettes

As the name implies, these are individual quiches.

Serves 6 (see p67 and back cover)

225g/8oz fine wholewheat flour
4 large sprigs parsley, finely chopped
125g/4oz butter or margarine
water to mix
½ green pepper, finely diced
½ red pepper, finely diced
1 small onion, finely chopped
125g/4oz roquefort cheese, crumbled
125ml/5fl oz milk
2 eggs, beaten
125ml/5fl oz soured cream
salt and pepper

1 Preheat the conventional oven to gas mark 5/ 190°C/375°F. Lightly grease 6 small deep quiche tins, approx 10cm/4in in diameter.

2 Place the flour and parsley in a mixing bowl. Rub in the butter or margarine until the mixture resembles fine breadcrumbs. Add sufficient water to bind the pastry into a firm dough.

3 Turn the pastry onto a floured board and knead lightly. Roll out and use to line the prepared tins.

4 Place the peppers and onion in a small covered microwave dish and cook for 3–4min, stirring once. Divide between the prepared quiche tins, adding the roquefort cheese.

5 Heat the milk for 2min in the microwave, then

add the eggs and soured cream and beat well. Add a little salt and pepper and pour the mixture into the quiches.

6 Place the individual tins on a baking sheet and bake in the preheated oven for 30–35min or until set and golden brown. Allow to stand for 10min, then serve warm or allow to cool completely.

Chef's tip: Quiches are much better if the pastry is cooked with the filling, instead of being previously baked blind. The best results are achieved by using metal quiche tins and placing them on a baking sheet in the oven to aid the cooking of the base of the pastry.

Serving suggestion: Serve warm with new potatoes, cooked in the microwave, or conventionally boiled potatoes, and green beans, broccoli or spinach cooked in the microwave.

Freezer storage life: 4 months. However, I prefer not to freeze quiches as they do tend to separate and become watery during storage.

To defrost: Quiches are best thawed slowly in the refrigerator, preferably for 3–4hr, to allow the defrosting to be as gentle as possible, thus minimising the tendency for the filling to separate.

Baked Potatoes

By combining the microwave with the conventional oven you can achieve quickly prepared baked potatoes with crispy skins.

Serves 2

2 large potatoes, approx 275g/10oz each, scrubbed and scored
butter
grated cheese, prawns, etc

1 Preheat the conventional oven to gas mark 7/ 210°C/425°F.
2 Place the potatoes in the microwave and cook for 8–12min until almost cooked.
3 Insert a metal skewer through each potato and place them in the preheated oven for 15–20min until the skins are crispy.
4 Slit the potatoes and add butter and the filling of your choice.

Freezer storage life: 6 months, unfilled.

To defrost: Heat each potato for 8–10min on 50%, then allow to stand for 5–10min.

To reheat: Heat for 5–8min on 100%.

Nasi Goreng

Nasi Goreng originated in the Far East, in Malaya and Indonesia. Adapted to Western cooking, it makes a quick-to-prepare supper dish and is a good way of using up left-over meat from a joint. Cooked beef or pork could be used instead of chicken.

Serves 4 (opposite)

225g/8oz long grain rice
500ml/1pt boiling water
3×15ml/tbsp oil, peanut or sunflower
1 large onion, finely chopped
1 clove garlic, crushed
½×5ml/tsp chilli powder
1×5ml/tsp ground cumin
½ small red pepper, cut into strips
½ small green pepper, cut into strips
125g/4oz mushrooms, thickly sliced
125g/4oz cooked chicken or duck
125g/4oz peeled prawns
salt and pepper

Omelette
1×15ml/tbsp oil
4 spring onions, trimmed and sliced
½×5ml/tsp chilli powder
4 eggs, beaten
salt

1 Place the rice and water in a large bowl and cook, covered, for 12–15min. Allow the rice to stand until required.
2 Heat the oil in a microwave serving dish for 2min, add the onion, garlic, chilli powder and cumin and cook for 3–4min, stirring once.
3 Add the sliced peppers and the mushrooms and cook for a further 3–4min, covered. Add the chicken or duck and cook for a further 3min.
4 Stir the rice and prawns into the mixture. Heat, uncovered, for 4–5min while preparing the omelette.
5 Heat the oil for the omelette in a large frying pan, add the onions and chilli powder and cook until the onions are softened. Add the beaten eggs with a little salt and cook until the omelette is almost set. Toss the omelette over and cook the other side.
6 Shred the omelette finely and serve over the rice.

Serving suggestion: Traditionally, this would be served with a bean dish and a peanut sauce. For a light lunch or supper dish serve the Nasi Goreng accompanied by a side salad.
Do not freeze.

Pasta with Mussels & Mushrooms

Very quick to prepare, this dish looks especially effective if made with multi-coloured pasta.

Serves 4 (see p55)

225g/8oz pasta spirals
1×15ml/tbsp oil
salt
25g/1oz butter
1 onion, finely sliced
1 clove garlic, crushed
225g/8oz button mushrooms, sliced
1×15ml/tbsp freshly chopped tarragon
    or basil
325g/12oz mussels, defrosted or canned
pepper
250ml/10fl oz soured cream
chopped tarragon or basil to garnish

1 Bring a large pan of water to the boil, add the pasta, oil and a pinch of salt and cook for 10–12min, or as directed on the packet.
2 Melt the butter in a large microwave dish for 1–2min, add the onion and garlic, cover and cook for 4min, stirring once.
3 Add the sliced mushrooms and the tarragon or basil and cook for a further 3–4min, covered, stirring once.
4 Stir the mussels into the dish and cook for 3–4min, until the mussels are hot.
5 Add the soured cream, stir well and season to taste. Heat for 2–3min on 70% until piping hot.
6 Drain the pasta and combine with the mussel and mushroom sauce. Serve garnished with freshly chopped tarragon or basil.

Chef's tip: Both tarragon and basil are traditionally used in tomato based dishes but can be used with all types of pasta. Chopped parsley may be used as an alternative.

Serving suggestion: Serve with herb bread (see p17) and a crisp side salad.

Freezer storage life: 2 months. Do not freeze if using defrosted, previously frozen mussels.

To defrost: Heat for 12–15min on 50%, then allow to stand for 10–15min.

To reheat: Heat for 10–12min on 70%.

Nasi Goreng (above)

Cauliflower & Prawn Au Gratin

Serves 4

1 large cauliflower, cut into florets
salt
40g/1½oz butter or margarine
40g/1½oz flour
375ml/15fl oz milk
4 slices bread
2 tomatoes, skinned, seeded and chopped
225g/8oz prawns
1×15ml/tbsp freshly chopped tarragon
    or parsley
75g/3oz gruyère cheese, grated
pepper

1 Bring a large pan of water to the boil, add the prepared cauliflower and a pinch of salt and simmer for 8–10min, until just tender.
2 Meanwhile, melt the butter in a large bowl or jug, add the flour and whisk well. Gradually whisk in the milk and heat for 5–6min until boiling and thickened, whisking every minute.
3 While the sauce is cooking, preheat the grill and toast the bread on both sides. Remove the crusts and cut into triangles.
4 Add the tomatoes, prawns, tarragon or parsley and 50g/2oz of the cheese to the sauce. Season to taste with salt and pepper.
5 Drain the cauliflower and place in a serving dish. Pour the sauce over and sprinkle with the remaining cheese. Brown under the hot grill for 2–3min.
6 Serve garnished with the toast triangles.

Chef's tip: The cauliflower may be cooked in the microwave and left to stand while the sauce is prepared. However, cooking it on the hob while the microwave is used for the sauce will speed the preparation time of this dish.

Serving suggestion: Serve with a small side salad.

Freezer storage life: 3 months. Do not freeze if made with previously frozen prawns.

To defrost: Heat for 15–20min on 50%, then allow to stand for 15–20min.

To reheat: Heat for 8–10min on 70%.

Mousagne

If you're a fan of moussaka and lasagne and can't decide which to cook, try this delicious combination of the two.

Serves 6

1 large onion, finely sliced
1 clove garlic, crushed
450g/1lb minced lamb
2×15ml/tbsp fresh oregano, chopped or
    2×5ml/tsp dried oregano

salt and freshly ground black pepper
1×15ml/tbsp tomato paste
400g/14oz can chopped tomatoes
2 aubergines, sliced
4×15ml/tbsp olive oil (optional)
25g/1oz butter
25g/1oz flour
250ml/10fl oz milk
225g/8oz fresh lasagne or easy-cook lasagne
125g/4oz feta cheese, cut into small pieces
2×15ml/tbsp parmesan cheese

1 Place the onion and garlic in a large covered microwave casserole dish and cook for 2–3min. Add the minced lamb and cook for a further 4min, covered, stirring once.
2 Add the oregano, salt and pepper, tomato paste and chopped tomatoes. Stir well, then cover and cook for 10min. Leave covered until required.
3 Preheat the conventional oven to gas mark 5/ 190°C/375°F.
4 Place the aubergines in a large microwave-to-oven casserole dish with the olive oil. Cover the dish and cook for 8–10min until soft. If preferred, the aubergine slices may be fried on the hob.
5 Prepare the sauce by melting the butter in a large jug in the microwave for 1–2min. Add the flour and stir well then gradually stir in the milk. Heat for 4–5min, uncovered, stirring every minute, until the sauce is boiling and thickened. Season to taste with salt and pepper.
6 Remove half the aubergine slices from the casserole and reserve. Place half the lasagne over the aubergines and top with all the minced lamb. Layer the rest of the lasagne over the meat and top with the remaining aubergine slices.
7 Pour the sauce over the mousagne and scatter the feta cheese over with the parmesan. If the dish is very full, place it on a baking sheet to prevent spills in the oven.
8 Bake in the preheated oven for 45–50min.

Chef's tip: Fresh or easy-cook lasagne which requires no pre-cooking is much easier to use than the conventionally dried sheets of pasta which tend to stick together during boiling.

Serving suggestion: Serve hot with a side salad. Mousagne is very filling and will only require a leafy green salad to accompany.

Freezer storage life: 4 months.

To defrost: Heat for 20–25min on 50%, then allow to stand for 10–15min.

To reheat: Heat for 12–15min on 70%.

Minced Beef & Mushroom Curry

Many quick curries have no authentic flavour as traditional ingredients are sacrificed for ease and speed of cooking. This recipe gives a well-flavoured curry, prepared in under 30min.

Serves 3

225g/8oz long grain rice
salt
500ml/1pt water
3×15ml/tbsp ghee or olive oil
1 large onion, finely sliced
1 clove garlic, crushed
1×15ml/tbsp ground coriander
1×5ml/tsp ground cinnamon
1×5ml/tsp turmeric
1×5ml/tsp ground ginger
½×5ml/tsp ground chilli
450g/1lb minced beef
225g/8oz mushrooms, sliced
3×15ml/tbsp tomato paste
salt and pepper

1 Place the rice, a pinch of salt and the water in a saucepan. Bring to the boil, then cover and simmer for 20min or until all the water is absorbed.
2 While the rice is cooking, heat the ghee or olive oil in a microwave casserole dish for 2–3min. Add the onion and garlic and cook for 3–4min.
3 Add the spices and cook for a further 2min.
4 Stir the minced beef into the spiced onion and cook, covered, for 4min, stirring once.
5 Add the sliced mushrooms, tomato paste and salt and pepper. Cover the dish and cook for a further 10min, stirring once during cooking.
6 Allow the rice to stand for 5min, covered, once all the water has been absorbed. Serve the rice with the curry.

Chef's tip: Curry spices should always be cooked in hot fat to avoid the floury, unroasted flavour that they sometimes assume.

Serving suggestion: Serve with mango chutney and poppadoms. Poppadoms can be cooked in the microwave, allowing 45–60sec each. They are best purchased, made in India, from an Indian shop.

Freezer storage life: 3 months.

To defrost: Heat for 10–12min on 50%, then allow to stand for 10min.

To reheat: Heat for 12–15min in a serving dish, with the rice around the outside of the curry.

Spaghetti with Aubergines & Lentils

This vegetarian spaghetti dish is bright, colourful and appetising.

Serves 4

4×15ml/tbsp oil
1 large onion, finely chopped
1 clove garlic, crushed
½ small red pepper, chopped
½ small green pepper, chopped
1 large aubergine, sliced
225g/8oz orange lentils
400g/14oz can chopped tomatoes
250ml/10fl oz boiling stock
salt and pepper
1×5ml/tsp dried mixed herbs
225–275g/8–10oz spaghetti
parmesan cheese to serve

1 Heat 3×15ml/tbsp of the oil in a large microwave bowl for 2min, add the onion and garlic and cook, covered, for 2–3min. Add the chopped peppers and cook for a further 2–3min.
2 Stir the aubergine into the vegetables and cook for 6–8min, or until soft, stirring once.
3 Add the lentils, tomatoes, stock, salt and pepper and herbs. Cover the dish and cook for 20min, stirring once during cooking.
4 While the sauce is cooking bring a large pan of water to the boil on the hob. Add a pinch of salt and 1×15ml/tbsp oil, then add the spaghetti. Simmer for 10min, or as directed on the packet.
5 Drain the spaghetti. Season the sauce to taste and serve over the spaghetti, sprinkled with parmesan cheese.

Freezer storage life: 6 months for the sauce.

To defrost: Heat for 12–15min on 50%, then allow to stand for 10min.

To reheat: Heat for 6–8min on 100%, stirring once or twice. Serve with freshly cooked spaghetti.

German Sausage Loaves

Infinitely better than hot dogs!

Serves 4 (opposite)

450g/1lb strong plain flour
1×5ml/tsp salt
75g/3oz butter or margarine
25g/1oz caster sugar
15g/½oz fresh yeast or
    1 sachet easy-blend dried yeast
175–200ml/7–8fl oz milk
1 egg, beaten
1×15ml/tbsp caraway seeds
2 german sausages, approx 225g/8oz each
2×15ml/tbsp mustard
beaten egg and caraway seeds to glaze

1 Place the flour and salt in a bowl and rub in the butter or margarine. If using easy-blend dried yeast, add the sugar and the yeast to the bowl.
2 Heat the milk for 45–60sec until tepid. If using fresh yeast, cream the yeast with 1×5ml/tsp sugar and a little of the milk. Add the remaining sugar to the bowl.
3 Make a well in the centre of the flour, add the beaten egg, the yeast liquid if using fresh yeast, and sufficient of the milk to form a soft manageable dough. Knead well until smooth and elastic.
4 Place the dough in a large bowl and cover. Heat for 15sec, then allow to stand for 5–10min. Repeat this process 4–5 times or until the dough has doubled in size.
5 Turn the dough onto a lightly floured surface, scatter with the caraway seeds and gently reknead until the seeds are evenly distributed throughout the dough. Divide into two.
6 Lightly grease 2 large baking sheets. Remove the skin from the sausages.
7 Roll each piece of dough to a shape just large enough to wrap round one of the sausages. Spread each sausage with 1×15ml/tbsp mustard, then roll in the dough. Place on a baking sheet with the join underneath the roll.
8 Cover the breads and leave in a warm place to rise for 45min.
9 Preheat the oven to gas mark 6/200°C/400°F.
10 Brush the loaves with beaten egg, then make 3–4 slits in each with a sharp knife. Scatter a few extra caraway seeds onto each loaf.
11 Bake in the preheated oven for 30–35min.

Chef's tip: Skin the sausages by running a sharp knife down the length of the sausage then simply peeling back the skin.

Serving suggestion: Serve hot or cold, with a mixed salad and german mustard.

Freezer storage life: 3 months.

To defrost: Heat each loaf for 8–10min on 50%, then allow to stand for 15min.

To reheat: Heat each loaf for 4–5min on 100%, uncovered.

Supper; left to right: German Sausage Loaves (above), Stuffed Mushrooms (page 13)

Main Course Medley

Main Course Medley covers a wide selection of recipes using meat, fish and eggs. Detailed serving suggestions are given and the emphasis is on using the recipes as part of a complete meal.

Microwave cooked fish is superb as it cooks very quickly and retains all its flavour and moisture. Many fish recipes require no cooking in addition to the microwave but the recipes in this section show how the grill or the oven can be used to complement the microwave for fish cookery.

In the selection of meat and game recipes, the microwave is used mainly in conjunction with the oven and the grill. For the smaller cuts of meat that are traditionally grilled, it is better to continue to grill them and to use the microwave to prepare sauces, gravies and vegetables, rather than to try to cook the whole dish in the microwave. This is especially true if cooking for a family.

Smaller cuts of meat are best cooked in a browning dish if they are to be microwaved. Do remember that just as you would brown them quickly under a grill and then lower the heat to finish cooking, so you should brown both sides in the browning dish on 100%, then complete the cooking on 70% to tenderise the meat.

As a general rule for casseroles, I prefer to start white meats, eg chicken and pork, on the hob and then complete the cooking in the microwave, whereas I find red meats, ie beef and lamb, best finished in the conventional oven after an initial cooking period in the microwave cooker. This tends to give the best visual result and an improved texture and flavour within a shorter cooking period than would be required conventionally. As a general rule it is fair to say that cheap cuts of red meats are not as satisfactory when cooked in the microwave as when cooked in a slow conventional oven.

Throughout this section there are suggestions for vegetables to accompany the dishes. It will sometimes be necessary to cook one vegetable on the hob to avoid a lot of last-minute reheating, but many items can be placed in a moderate oven to keep warm without risk of spoiling.

See also Roast Stuffed Shoulder of Lamb (p101), Venison with Juniper & Peppercorns (p108), Wild Duck with Pear & Lemon Sauce (p112), Stuffed Salmon en Croute with Hollandaise Sauce (p115), Chicken & Tomato Casserole (p100), Cod and Potato Pie (p98), and Calves' Liver in Brandy & Cream (p113).

Smoked Fillet of Pork with Pineapple & Tarragon Sauce

Serves 4 (see p79)

1 smoked fillet of pork, approx 900g/2lb
400g/14oz puff pastry, defrosted
1×15ml/tbsp semolina
1 egg, beaten
1 medium onion, finely chopped
1×225g/8oz can pineapple in natural
    juice, puréed
1×15ml/tbsp freshly chopped tarragon
salt and pepper
125ml/5fl oz soured cream or natural yogurt
fresh tarragon to garnish

1 Cook the pork fillet on a microwave roasting rack, allowing 10min per 450g/lb at 70%. Turn the fillet over half way through cooking to prevent drying.
2 Meanwhile, preheat the conventional oven to gas mark 7/210°C/425°F.
3 Roll out the pastry on a lightly floured board to a

large rectangle, approx 35.5×30.5cm/14×12in. Brush the edges of the pastry with beaten egg.

3 Place the pork fillet in the centre of the pastry, reserving the juices in the roasting dish. Sprinkle the semolina on the joint, then fold the pastry around the fillet and seal the edges.

4 Run a baking sheet under cold water and place the pastry-covered fillet on it with all seams under the joint. Brush with beaten egg. Roll out any remaining pastry and cut into leaves for decoration.

5 Bake in the preheated oven for 20–25min or until the pastry is golden brown.

6 Prepare the sauce in the microwave. Cook the onion in a covered dish with any juices from the pork for 3min on 100%, then add the puréed pineapple and the tarragon with a little salt and pepper. Cook for 8–10min until reduced and thickened. Season to taste and allow to cool slightly before adding the cream or yogurt. Reheat for 1–2min.

7 Carve the pork into thick slices and serve with the sauce.

Chef's tip: A little semolina absorbs cooking juices when baking en croute and prevents the pastry under the filling from becoming soggy.

Serving suggestion: Serve with Sauté Potatoes (p61), Stuffed Tomatoes (p69) and Leeks with Almonds (p62). Cook the almonds and the potatoes in advance. Prepare and stuff the tomatoes. Prepare the pork fillet and bake in the oven. Immediately cook the sauce and set aside to reheat at the last minute. Cook the tomatoes, then finish slowly under the grill. Cook the leeks, then reheat the sauce for 2–3min. Serve.

Freezer storage life: 3 months. Do not freeze the pineapple sauce.

To defrost: Heat for 20–25min on 30%, then allow to stand for 20min.

To reheat: Reheat the pork fillet conventionally, otherwise the pastry will become soggy. Heat, sliced, for 15–20min at gas mark 5/190°C/375°F. This dish is definitely better when freshly cooked.

Galantine of Chicken

A perfect dish for a Glyndebourne-style picnic, which I first made for a Goodwood Hamper.

Serves 6 (see p83)

1×2–2½kg/4–5lb chicken, boned completely
3 slices ox tongue, weighing 50g/2oz each
1 onion, finely chopped
225g/8oz minced pork
1×10ml/dsp freshly chopped sage (optional)
salt and pepper
3×15ml/tbsp clear honey
grated rind 1 lemon
2×15ml/tbsp chopped tarragon

1 Prepare the chicken. Using a very sharp knife, remove the wing and leg tips and cut down the backbone, carefully easing all the meat from the rib-cage. Cut through the ball and socket joints of the wings and the thighs. Scrape the meat from the thighs, drumsticks and wings and remove the bones. Carefully remove the rib cage from the chicken, taking great care not to split the skin on the breast. The bones may all be used for stock or soup.

2 Lay the chicken on a board and spread the tongue slices, cut into small pieces, over the meat.

3 Place the onion in a small covered bowl and microwave for 2min. Allow to cool, then mix with the minced pork, sage, salt and pepper. Pile into the centre of the chicken, then sew the chicken into a roll, using a trussing needle and string.

4 Weigh the stuffed and trussed chicken and cook on a rack in the microwave at 70% allowing 8min per 450g/lb.

5 Preheat the conventional oven to gas mark 5/190°C/375°F. Transfer the chicken to a small roasting tin.

6 Place the honey and lemon rind in a small bowl and heat for 1–1½min in the microwave at 100%. Add the chopped tarragon and brush the glaze over the chicken. Cook in the preheated oven for 30min or until the skin is browned and crispy, basting occasionally.

7 Allow to cool, then chill well before serving.

Chef's tip: Boning a chicken is not as difficult as it sounds – a small sharp knife is the most important piece of equipment. Carefully cut all the meat away from the bones, following the way in which the joints fall away from the rib-cage in the centre of the chicken.

Serving suggestion: Carve the galantine into thick slices and serve with a green or tomato salad and brown bread and butter.

Freezer storage life: 3 months.

To defrost: Heat for 15min at 30%, then allow to stand for 1–1½hr. Chill in the refrigerator.

Gammon Steaks with Cucumber & Soured Cream Sauce

The idea for this recipe came from a discussion over hotel menus in one of my favourite radio programmes.

Serves 4 (opposite)

½ cucumber, peeled and diced
salt and pepper
4–5 slices dill cucumber, diced
4 gammon steaks, approx 125–150g/4–5oz each
125g/4oz butter
2×15ml/tbsp vinegar from dill cucumbers
2 egg yolks
125ml/5fl oz soured cream
1×15ml/tbsp freshly chopped chives

1 Place the prepared cucumber in a colander, sprinkling each layer generously with salt. Leave for approx 1hr. Rinse the cucumber well under running water.
2 Preheat the conventional grill and cook the gammon steaks for approx 6min, turning once.
3 While the gammon is cooking, place the cucumber and the dill cucumber in a covered bowl and cook for 3–4min in the microwave, stirring once. Leave covered.
4 Heat the butter in a bowl or jug for 1min or until melted. Add the vinegar and the egg yolks and whisk well. Heat for approx 2min at 50%, whisking every 15–30sec until thick and glossy.
5 Add the soured cream and chives, and season to taste with salt and pepper.
6 Serve the gammon steaks with the sauce poured over, accompanied by the diced cucumbers.

Chef's tip: Grill the gammon steaks slowly as they will very easily dry out if cooked too quickly. The sauce is based on the classic hollandaise sauce and must be prepared at the last moment and then served immediately.

Serving suggestion: Serve with Sauté Potatoes (p61), Stuffed Tomatoes (p69) and a small green salad. Cook the potatoes in the microwave before beginning the preparation of the gammon, then fry on the hob. Prepare and stuff the tomatoes, then heat in the microwave. At the same time, preheat the grill. Grill the gammon, then finish the tomatoes under the grill while the sauce is being prepared in the microwave.
Do not freeze.

Pork with Fresh Herbs

This recipe was originally developed as a good way of using up homemade wine.

Serves 6 (opposite)

900g/2lb boneless shoulder of pork
salt
2×15ml/tbsp seasoned flour
2 onions, finely sliced
2 carrots, cut into matchsticks
4 rashers rinded streaky bacon, diced
4×15ml/tbsp freshly chopped mixed herbs
2 bay leaves
freshly ground black pepper
250ml/10fl oz white wine, approx
3×5ml/tsp cornflour
125ml/5fl oz soured cream
freshly chopped mixed herbs to garnish

1 Remove the crackling from the pork and score deeply. Rub with salt and put to one side.
2 Cut the meat into 2.5cm/1in pieces and toss in the seasoned flour.
3 Place the onion, carrot and bacon in a covered microwave-to-oven casserole and cook for 4–5min, stirring once. Add the pork and cook for a further 6min, stirring once.
4 Add the herbs, bay leaves and some salt and pepper, then gradually add the wine (use sufficient to cover the meat). Cover and cook for 10min on 100%, stir, then reduce the power to 50% and cook for a further 15min.
5 Whilst the casserole is cooking, preheat the conventional oven to gas mark 3/160°C/325°F. Transfer the casserole to the oven and cook for a further 45min, or until the meat is tender.
6 Pat the crackling dry with kitchen paper. Place on a microwave roasting rack and cook for approx 10min, until well crackled. Chop.
7 Blend the cornflour with a little of the liquor from the casserole, then stir into the dish. Cover and return to the oven for a further 15min.
8 Remove the bay leaves from the casserole and season to taste. Stir in the soured cream and sprinkle with the chopped crackling and freshly chopped mixed herbs before serving.

Chef's tip: In a dish which is relying on herbs for its main flavour, it is especially important to get

top to bottom: Pork with Fresh Herbs (above), Gammon Steaks with Cucumber & Soured Cream Sauce (above), Greek-style Bean Ratatouille (page 65)

the most from each of the herbs. Chop the herbs with a knife rather than in a blender as less flavour is lost in liquid produced by the very fast chopping action of the machine. Bay leaves must be broken before being added to the casserole to allow the maximum flavour to be released from the leaves. I prefer to use dried bay leaves as fresh can be rather bitter.

Serving suggestion: Serve with conventionally boiled pasta, Apple & Aubergine Ratatouille (p70) and a green vegetable of your choice. Cook the ratatouille, then place it in the oven, with the pork, to keep warm, while cooking the green vegetable in the microwave.

Freezer storage life: 3 months. Do not add the crackling as it will soften in the casserole.

To defrost: Heat for 20min on 30%, then allow to stand for 15–20min.

To reheat: Heat for 10–12min on 70%, stirring once.

Lamb Chops with Kumquat Sauce

Kumquats are tiny oranges and are one of the range of exotic fruits now widely available in our supermarkets.

Serves 2

4 lamb chops, trimmed
salt and pepper
1 small onion, finely chopped
175g/6oz kumquats, washed
½×15ml/tbsp freshly chopped rosemary
250ml/10fl oz orange juice
demerara sugar to taste

1 Preheat the conventional grill. Season the chops and brown them on both sides under the grill.
2 Meanwhile, cook the onion in a covered dish, in the microwave, for 2–3min. Add the kumquats, salt and pepper, chopped rosemary and orange juice. Cover and cook for 5min.
3 Add the chops to the sauce with any meat juices and cook for a further 10–15min at 30% until the chops are tender.
4 Remove the chops to a warm serving plate. Liquidise or purée the sauce and season to taste, adding sugar if required.
5 Serve the chops with the sauce.

Chef's tip: Kumquats may be eaten whole as a fruit, including the skin, but do not swallow the pips.

Serving suggestion: Serve with boiled potatoes, cooked on the hob, and a green vegetable. Cook the vegetable in the microwave while liquidising the sauce.

Freezer storage life: 3 months.

To defrost: Heat for 10–12min on 30%, then allow to stand for 10min.

To reheat: Heat for 6–8min on 70%.

Aubergine & Fish Lasagne

The combination of haddock, prawns and aubergine makes a good variation on the traditional filling of minced beef.

Serves 6

1 medium aubergine, approx 325g/12oz
salt
500ml/1pt milk
6 peppercorns
1 bay leaf
2 blades mace
2×15ml/tbsp oil
1 large onion, finely sliced
400g/14oz can chopped tomatoes
1×15ml/tbsp tomato paste
salt and freshly ground black pepper
½×5ml/tsp dried basil
350g/12oz haddock, skinned and
  cut into 5cm/2in pieces
125g/4oz mushrooms, thickly sliced
125g/4oz peeled prawns
125g/4oz fresh or easy-cook lasagne
40g/1½oz butter
50g/2oz butter or margarine
50g/2oz flour
25g/1oz grated parmesan cheese

1 Wash and trim the aubergine. Slice finely and layer in a dish, liberally sprinkled with salt. Leave for about 20min.
2 Add the peppercorns, bay leaf and mace to the milk and heat for 5min. Cover and leave to stand.
3 Preheat the conventional oven to gas mark 5/ 190°C/375°F.
4 Heat the oil in a large microwave dish for 2min, add the onion, cover and cook for 3min. Add the chopped tomatoes, tomato paste and seasonings and cook for 5min, stirring once.
5 Add the haddock and mushrooms to the tomato

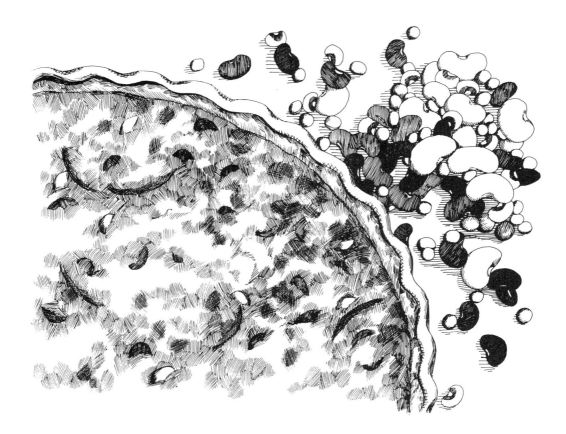

mixture, cover and cook for 5min, then stir in the prawns.

6 Rinse and drain the aubergine slices and pat dry. Melt 40g/1½oz butter in a small frying pan on the hob and cook the aubergine slices until browned on both sides.

7 Place half the aubergine slices in the bottom of a large shallow ovenproof dish, layer half the lasagne over the aubergine, then cover with half the fish and tomato mixture. Repeat the layers with the remaining ingredients.

8 Melt 50g/2oz butter or margarine in the microwave. Heat in a large jug for 2min, then stir in the flour. Strain the milk and gradually add it to the jug, beating well. Heat for 5–6min, stirring every minute, until boiling and thickened. Correct the seasoning and pour the sauce over the lasagne.

9 Sprinkle the parmesan over the dish and bake in the preheated oven for 40–45min until browned.

Serving suggestion: Serve with Braised Celery (p72).

Freezer storage life: 3 months.

To defrost: Heat for 20min on 50%, then allow to stand for 10–15min.

To reheat: Heat for 15min on 70%.

Spiced Bean Quiche

A most substantial quiche.

Serves 6–8

125g/4oz mixed dried beans
boiling water

Pastry
225g/8oz fine wholewheat flour
pinch salt
125g/4oz margarine and lard, mixed
water to mix

Filling
2 large onions, finely chopped
1 clove garlic, crushed
2×15ml/tbsp oil
1×5ml/tsp chilli powder
2 tomatoes, sliced
4 eggs, beaten
375ml/15fl oz milk
4×15ml/tbsp fromage frais or soured cream
salt and pepper
few drops chilli or chilli and
    garlic sauce (optional)
50g/2oz cheddar cheese, grated

1 Place the beans in a microwave dish and cover with boiling water. Cover and cook for 5min, then allow to stand for 1hr. Drain and rinse the beans.

2 Return the beans to the dish and cover with fresh boiling water. Cover and cook for 10min at 100%, then a further 20–25min on 50%. Allow to stand until required.

3 Preheat the oven to gas mark 5/190°C/375°F. Lightly grease a 20cm/8in diameter deep quiche tin.

4 Place the flour and salt in a bowl and rub in the fat until the mixture resembles breadcrumbs. Add sufficient water to mix. Turn onto a floured board and knead lightly, then roll out and use to line the prepared quiche tin.

5 Place the onions, garlic, oil and chilli powder in a covered microwave dish and cook for 4–5min on 100%, stirring once. Drain the beans and mix with the onions, then place in the base of the quiche. Place the tomato slices over the bean mixture.

6 Beat together the eggs, milk and fromage frais or soured cream. Add a little salt and pepper and the chilli sauce if used, then pour the mixture into the pastry shell.

7 Sprinkle the grated cheese over the quiche and place the quiche tin on a baking sheet. Bake in the preheated oven for 45min or until set. Allow to cool for 10min, then serve warm or allow to cool completely.

Serving suggestion: Serve with new potatoes, cooked in the microwave, or boiled potatoes, cooked on the hob, and a mixed salad or a freshly cooked vegetable in season.

Freezer storage life: 4 months, but quiches tend to separate during freezing.

To defrost: Allow to defrost slowly, overnight or for 4–5hr, in the refrigerator.

To reheat: Heat for 20min in the conventional oven at gas mark 5/190°C/375°F. Reheating in the microwave will cause the pastry to become soggy.

Roast Pheasants with Orange & Chestnuts

A dish for a very special occasion.

Serves 4 (opposite)

1 brace pheasants, dressed
4 rashers bacon
40g/1½oz butter
1×10ml/dsp wholewheat flour

Marinade
1 large onion, finely sliced
6 juniper berries

6 peppercorns
1×15ml/tbsp mustard seed
2 bay leaves
3×15ml/tbsp wine vinegar
100ml/4fl oz gin
250ml/10fl oz orange juice, approx

Sauce
50g/2oz butter
1 onion, finely chopped
450g/1lb chestnuts, skinned or
    175g/6oz dried chestnuts
salt and pepper
100ml/4fl oz gin
2×15ml/tbsp demerara sugar

watercress to garnish

1 Place the onion in the bottom of a casserole dish, then place the pheasants on top. Choose a dish in which the pheasants will fit tightly.

2 Add the juniper berries, peppercorns, mustard seeds, bay leaves and vinegar, then pour the gin over. Add sufficient orange juice to cover the birds, cover the dish and marinade for at least 8hr, but preferably for 24hr. Turn the pheasants occasionally.

3 If using dried chestnuts in the sauce, place them in a bowl and cover with boiling water. Cover the bowl and heat for 5min in the microwave. Allow to stand for 1hr then drain.

4 Preheat the conventional oven to gas mark 8/250°C/450°F.

5 Remove the pheasants from the marinade and pat dry. Cut the birds in half lengthways for easy serving, using game shears or sharp scissors. Place in a roasting tin and cover the breasts with the bacon. Roast for 10min then reduce the heat to gas mark 6/200°C/400°F and roast for a further 30–40min.

6 Melt 40g/1½oz butter in the microwave for 1min and use to baste the breasts of the pheasants frequently.

7 Strain the marinade and measure the liquid – add extra orange juice, if necessary, to give 500ml/1pt.

8 Melt 50g/2oz butter in the microwave, add the onion and cook for 2min. Add the chestnuts, salt and pepper, and the marinade. Cook, uncovered, for 20–25min, until the nuts are soft.

9 15min before the end of the pheasants' cooking time, remove the bacon and sprinkle the flour over the pheasants. Return them to the oven.

10 Chop the bacon and add it to the sauce.

11 Heat the gin for the sauce for 30–40sec in a small jug in the microwave, remove the jug and ignite the gin. Allow the flames to subside, then

Roast Pheasants with Orange & Chestnuts (above)

add to the sauce, season to taste and add the sugar.

12 Serve the pheasants, garnished with watercress, with the sauce poured over, or handed separately.

Chef's tip: If using fresh chestnuts, prick them well and place 6 at a time in the microwave. Heat for 45–60sec, then skin the hot chestnuts before heating the next batch.

Serving suggestion: This is very rich so serve with a light starter and dessert. To accompany the pheasants, serve Sauté Potatoes (p61), cooked on the hob, carrots tossed in chopped parsley, and spinach. Cook the potatoes in advance in the microwave and sauté on the hob when required. Cook the sauce for the pheasants in advance, adding the bacon from the pheasants when available and reheating the sauce for 3–4min just before serving. Cook the carrots in the microwave and leave covered while reheating the sauce. Cook the spinach on the hob and serve with a knob of butter and plenty of black pepper.

Freezer storage life: 3 months. Do not freeze if using previously frozen game.

To defrost: Heat for 15–18min on 30%, then allow to stand for 10min.

To reheat: Heat for 15min on 70%, rearranging the pheasant quarters half way through heating.

Lamb with Dill & Caper Sauce

Grilled lamb served with a mildly herbed sauce in the mid-European style.

Serves 6 (see p95)

6 lamb shoulder cuts
salt and freshly ground black pepper
40g/1½oz butter
1 onion, finely chopped
50g/2oz dill cucumber, chopped
40g/1½oz flour
200ml/8fl oz milk
1×15ml/tbsp freshly chopped dill
1–2×15ml/tbsp capers
125ml/5fl oz soured cream
dill cucumber and capers to garnish

1 Preheat the grill and cook the lamb, allowing 15–20min according to the size of the cut and your preference for cooking.
2 Prepare the sauce while the lamb is cooking.

Melt the butter in a bowl for 1–2min, add the onion and chopped dill cucumber and cook, covered, for 4–5min, stirring once.
3 Add the flour and mix well, then gradually stir in the milk. Heat for 4–5min until thickened and boiling, then add the dill and capers. Cool slightly, then stir in the soured cream.
4 Season the sauce to taste, then heat for 1–2min on 70%.
5 Serve the sauce over the lamb, garnished with a few extra capers and dill cucumbers if required.

Chef's tip: Allow the sauce to cool slightly before adding the cream to prevent curdling.

Serving suggestion: Serve with creamed potatoes, cooked on the hob, or Pasta with Poppy Seeds (p69) and Braised Red Cabbage (p109) or fresh vegetables in season. Cook the sauce for the pasta first, then add it to the pasta and heat through on the hob before transferring to a preheated oven to keep warm. Cook the cabbage in the microwave, then transfer that to the oven until required. Start grilling the shoulder cuts towards the end of the red cabbage cooking period.

Freezer storage life: 3 months. Freeze meat and sauce separately.

To defrost: Heat the meat for 10–12min on 30%, then allow to stand for 10min. Heat the sauce for 4–5min on 50%, then allow to stand for 5min.

To reheat: Heat for 10min on 70%.

Raised Game Pie

The microwave cooker is used in the preparation of a hot water crust pie to prepare the pastry and the aspic.

Serves 6–8

Pastry
125ml/5fl oz water
125g/4oz lard, cut into small pieces
450g/1lb flour
2×5ml/tsp salt
3–4×15ml/tbsp water or milk

Filling
1 pheasant, approx 1kg/2½lb
1 wild duck, approx 675g/1½lb
1 large onion
salt and freshly ground black pepper
1×15ml/tbsp freshly chopped sage
2×15ml/tbsp redcurrant jelly

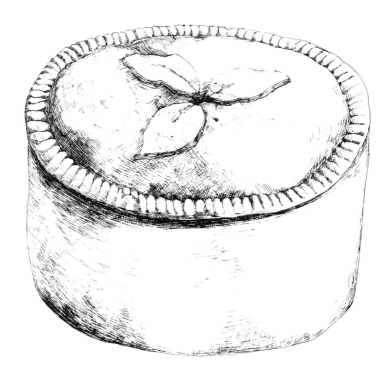

Glaze
1 egg, beaten
salt

Jelly
175ml/7fl oz water
15g/½oz aspic powder

1 Place the water and lard in a microwave mixing bowl and heat for 3–4min or until the lard has melted and the mixture is boiling.

2 Shoot in the flour and salt and beat well, adding the extra liquid as required to give a soft, workable dough. Knead lightly, then leave covered while preparing the filling.

3 Preheat the conventional oven to gas mark 7/210°C/425°F.

4 Carefully remove the breasts from the pheasant and one breast from the duck and set to one side. Cut the remaining meat from the carcasses and mince finely with the livers from the birds. Mince the onion and add to the meat.

5 Season the mince with salt and pepper, then add the chopped sage and redcurrant jelly.

6 Roll out two thirds of the pastry and use to line the base and sides of a 20cm/8in round spring-form, loose bottomed tin. Place half the mince in the bottom of the tin.

7 Lightly beat the reserved breasts with a steak hammer, then place in a layer in the tin. Top with the remaining mince.

8 Roll out the remaining pastry to a circle approx 24cm/9½in in diameter. Brush the rim with beaten egg and lay over the pie. Trim the edges, then seal the top to the sides of the pie, pinching together.

9 Brush the top of the pie with beaten egg. Roll out any pastry trimmings and cut into leaves or other shapes to garnish the pie. Brush with egg, then place on the pie.

10 Bake in the preheated oven for 15min, then reduce the temperature to gas mark 4/180°C/350°F and bake for a further 1hr.

11 Remove the pie from the tin. Add a little salt to the beaten egg and use to brush the sides and top of the pie. Return the pie to the oven for a further 40min, occasionally brushing with any remaining egg.

12 Allow the pie to cool completely.

13 Heat the water for the aspic in the microwave for 1min, add the aspic powder and stir well. Heat for a further 1min until dissolved, then allow to cool.

14 Carefully pour the aspic into the pie through the hole in the lid. Allow to set in the refrigerator for 2–3hr before serving.

Chef's tip: The pie is cooked if the meat feels tender when tested with a skewer. Insert the skewer through the hole in the top crust of the pie.

Serving suggestion: Serve cold with salads or pickles and hot Baked Potatoes (see p112).

Freezer storage life: 3 months.

To defrost: Allow to defrost overnight in the refrigerator.

Smoked Haddock Stuffed Canneloni

Smoked haddock and hard-boiled eggs combine well in this pasta dish.

Serves 6

4 eggs
450g/1lb smoked haddock
50g/2oz butter
1 large onion, chopped
50g/2oz flour
500ml/1pt milk
16–18 easy-cook canneloni tubes
125ml/5fl oz white wine
2×15ml/tbsp parmesan cheese
chopped parsley to garnish

1 Preheat the conventional oven to gas mark 6/ 200°C/400°F.
2 Place the eggs in a pan of water on the hob. Bring to the boil and cook for 8–10min. Drain the eggs and crack the shells immediately. Place the eggs in cold water.
3 Cook the smoked haddock in a covered dish for 5–6min. Allow to cool slightly, then skin and flake the fish.
4 Melt the butter for 1–2 min, add the onion and cook for 2–3min. Stir in the flour and add the milk. Cook for 8–10min until boiling and thickened, stirring every 1–2min. Season to taste.
5 Shell and chop the eggs, then mix with the haddock. Bind the filling together with 125ml/5fl oz of the sauce. Season to taste and use to fill the canneloni tubes.
6 Place the filled tubes in an ovenproof dish. Add 125ml/5fl oz of white wine to the remaining sauce. Season the sauce to taste and pour over the canneloni.
7 Sprinkle the dish with the parmesan cheese and bake in the preheated oven for 35–40min.

Chef's tip: The easiest way to fill the pasta tubes is to hold them upright in the serving dish and push the filling downwards with the handle of a 5ml/ teaspoon.

Serving suggestion: Serve with Braised Celery (p72) or a salad.

Freezer storage life: 3 months.

To defrost: Heat for 12–15min on 50%, then allow to stand for 10min.

To reheat: Heat for 10–12min on 70%.

Steak & Kidney Pudding

This traditional favourite does not require hours of steaming if you use the pressure cooker to cook the meat and then cook the suet crust in the microwave.

Serves 4–5 (opposite)

3×15ml/tbsp oil
2×15ml/tbsp flour
salt and pepper
675g/1½lb stewing steak, cut into large dice
450g/1lb kidney, cored and chopped
250ml/10fl oz water or stock
350g/12oz self-raising flour
175g/6oz shredded suet
water to mix

1 Heat the oil in the bottom of the pressure cooker. Season the flour with salt and pepper, add the prepared meat and toss in the flour. Add the meat to the pressure cooker and brown on all sides in the hot oil.
2 Pour the stock into the pan. Cover and bring the pan to 15lb/high pressure, according to the manufacturer's instructions. Cook the meat for 20min, then reduce the pressure.
3 Lightly grease a 1litre/2pt pudding basin. In a mixing bowl, mix together the flour and suet with a pinch of salt, then add sufficient cold water to form a soft dough.
4 Knead the dough lightly on a floured surface, then reserve one third of it for the lid of the pudding. Roll out the larger portion and use to line the bottom and sides of the pudding basin.
5 Remove the meat from the pressure cooker with a draining spoon and place in the lined basin. Roll out the remaining dough to a circle and damp the underside with water. Place over the pudding, sealing the edges of the dough together. Slit the top of the pudding with a sharp knife.
6 Place the pudding on a microwave rack and cover with a large mixing bowl or microwave film. Cook for 7–9min.
7 While the pudding is cooking, heat the gravy from the meat in the pressure cooker base. When the pudding is cooked, pour the gravy into the pudding and serve.

Serving suggestion: Serve with conventionally boiled potatoes and vegetables in season. The vegetables may be cooked in the microwave while

Steak & Kidney Pudding (above)

the meat is in the pressure cooker, left covered and then reheated for 2–3min before serving.

Freezer storage life: 3 months.

To defrost: Heat for 15–18min on 30%, then allow to stand for 15min.

To reheat: Heat for 10–12min on 70%.

Pork Goulash

This variation of the traditional Hungarian favourite is rich and full of flavour, and makes a good dinner party dish.

Serves 6

2 large onions, finely sliced
1–2 cloves garlic, crushed
2 large red peppers, cut into strips
2 large green peppers, cut into strips
900g/2lb boneless leg of pork, fat removed, trimmed and diced
3×15ml/tbsp wholewheat flour
3×15ml/tbsp paprika
3 bay leaves
2×15ml/tbsp tomato paste
2×15ml/tbsp wine vinegar
salt and freshly ground black pepper
500ml/1pt boiling chicken stock
325g/12oz chorizo sausage, sliced
1–2×15ml/tbsp demerara sugar
125ml/5fl oz soured cream

1 Place the onions, garlic and peppers in a large casserole dish, suitable for use in the microwave and the conventional oven. Cover and cook for 10–12min in the microwave until soft, stirring once.
2 Toss the pork in the flour and add to the casserole. Cook, covered, for 6–8min, stirring once. Add the paprika, bay leaves, tomato paste and vinegar.
3 Add the boiling stock, stirring continuously. Season with a little salt and black pepper, then cover the casserole and cook for 10min.
4 Preheat the conventional oven to gas mark 3/160°C/325°F. Stir the goulash and cook for a further 20min on 50%.
5 Add the sliced sausage to the goulash. Transfer the casserole to the preheated oven and cook for a further 1hr until the meat is tender.
6 Remove the bay leaves and add the sugar, then season to taste with salt and pepper. Stir in the soured cream and serve immediately.

Serving suggestion: Serve with conventionally boiled noodles and a green vegetable, eg green beans, runner beans or broccoli. Cook the vegetable in the microwave.

Freezer storage life: 3 months.

To defrost: Heat for 12–15min on 30%, then allow to stand for 20min.

To reheat: Heat for 10–12min on 70%.

Chicken with Stilton Sauce

Serves 6

6 chicken breasts, beaten flat
6 rashers rinded short back bacon
25g/1oz butter
2 large salad onions, trimmed and sliced
25g/1oz flour
125ml/5fl oz milk
125ml/5fl oz soured cream or set natural yogurt
75g/3oz stilton cheese, crumbled
watercress to garnish

1 Place the chicken breasts on a microwave roasting rack and cook for 10–12min on 70%. Preheat the grill.
2 Place a rasher of bacon on each chicken breast and grill slowly for approx 10min until the chicken is cooked through and the bacon is crispy.
3 While the chicken is cooking, melt the butter for 1–2min in a microwave bowl or jug. Add the onions, cover and cook for 1–2min then stir in the flour.
4 Gradually stir in the milk and heat for 3min, stirring every minute, until the sauce is thickened.
5 Stir the cream into the sauce and add the stilton. Heat for 1–2min, stirring every 30sec.
6 Season the sauce to taste and serve over the chicken breasts. Garnish with watercress.

Serving suggestion: Serve with boiled potatoes, cooked on the hob, and a mixed salad.

Freezer storage life: 3 months.

To defrost: Heat for 15–18min on 30%, then allow to stand for 20min.

To reheat: Heat the chicken and sauce separately, allowing 10–12min on 70% for the chicken, and 3–4min on 100% for the sauce. Stir the sauce once during heating.

Seafoods Supreme

A delicious combination of seafoods in a brandy and cream sauce.

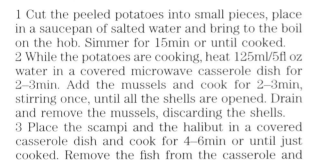

Serves 4–5

675g/1½lb potatoes, peeled
water
450g/1lb live mussels in shells, cleaned
175g/6oz unbreaded scampi
225–275g/8–10oz halibut steak
1 sherry glassful of brandy
250ml/10fl oz double or whipping cream
2 egg yolks
salt and pepper
225g/8oz peeled prawns
butter
milk
parsley to garnish

1 Cut the peeled potatoes into small pieces, place in a saucepan of salted water and bring to the boil on the hob. Simmer for 15min or until cooked.
2 While the potatoes are cooking, heat 125ml/5fl oz water in a covered microwave casserole dish for 2–3min. Add the mussels and cook for 2–3min, stirring once, until all the shells are opened. Drain and remove the mussels, discarding the shells.
3 Place the scampi and the halibut in a covered casserole dish and cook for 4–6min or until just cooked. Remove the fish from the casserole and allow to cool slightly before skinning the halibut and removing the bone. Divide the halibut into bite-size pieces.
4 Heat the brandy for 30sec, then remove from the microwave and ignite. Pour the liquid into the casserole with the fish juice and leave until the flames subside. Whisk in the cream and the egg yolks and heat for 5min on 50% until thickened, whisking frequently.
5 Season the sauce, then add the mussels, scampi, halibut and prawns. Heat for 4–5min on 50%, uncovered.
6 Preheat the conventional grill.
7 Drain the potatoes and purée in a liquidiser or processor with a knob of butter and a little milk. Spoon or pipe the potato around the edge of a serving dish and place the fish in cream sauce in the centre.
8 Brown the top of the potatoes and sauce under the grill, then serve garnished with fresh parsley.

Chef's tip: Potatoes that are to be piped need to be processed to a fine purée to ensure that there are no lumps that will block the forcing tube.

Serving suggestion: Serve with a salad or asparagus for a special occasion. Cook the asparagus in the microwave while the seafoods are being browned under the grill.
Do not freeze.

Pasta with Spicy Sausage

Serves 3 (opposite)

225g/8oz wholewheat pasta shells
1×15ml/tbsp oil
salt
25g/1oz butter or margarine
1 onion, finely sliced
50g/2oz mushrooms, sliced
25g/1oz flour
250ml/10fl oz milk
freshly ground black pepper
225g/8oz spicy sausage, eg chorizo, skinned and diced
2×15ml/tbsp parmesan cheese

1 Bring a large pan of water to the boil on the hob. Add the pasta shells, oil and a pinch of salt. Cook for 12min, or as directed on the packet.
2 While the pasta is cooking, melt the butter or margarine in a large dish in the microwave for 1–2min. Add the onion and cook, covered, for 2–3min. Add the mushrooms and cook for a further 2min. Remove the onion and mushroom from the dish with a slotted spoon and reserve until required.
3 Stir the flour into the juices in the dish and blend well. Gradually add the milk, then heat for 4–5min, until boiling and thickened. Stir every minute.
4 Season the sauce to taste, then add the onion and mushroom mixture and the diced spicy sausage.
5 Drain the pasta and add to the sauce. Stir well then transfer to a microwave serving dish, suitable for use under the grill. Heat in the microwave for 5min at 70%.
6 While the pasta is heating in the microwave, preheat the grill.
7 Sprinkle the pasta with the parmesan cheese and brown under the hot grill.

Chef's tip: Some of the pasta will become crispy under the grill – this adds an interesting texture to the dish.

Serving suggestion: Serve with a leafy green salad.

Freezer storage life: 3 months.

To defrost: Heat for 12–15min at 50%, then allow to stand for 10–15min.

To reheat: Heat for 10–12min at 70%.

Devilled Kidneys with Pasta

Serves 2–3 (opposite)

450g/1lb lambs' kidneys, cored and sliced
3×15ml/tbsp oil
salt and cayenne pepper
125g/4oz mushrooms, thickly sliced
175g/6oz pasta
25g/1oz butter
25g/1oz flour
250ml/10fl oz milk, approx
parsley or cayenne pepper to garnish

1 Place the kidneys in a large dish and add 2×15ml/tbsp oil, a little salt and cayenne pepper. Cover and cook for 4min, stirring once. Add the mushrooms and cook for a further 5min, covered, at 70%.
2 Meanwhile, bring a pan of water to the boil on the hob and add a pinch of salt and 1×15ml/tbsp oil. Add the pasta and cook as directed on the packet.
3 Melt the butter in a large jug for 1–2min, add the flour and mix well. Drain any juices from the kidneys and mushrooms and make up to 250ml/10fl oz with milk. Gradually add the liquid and cook for 4–5min until boiling and thickened, stirring every minute.
4 Add the kidneys to the sauce and season to taste.
5 Drain the pasta and serve, topped with the kidneys in the sauce. Garnish with parsley or sprinkle with a little extra cayenne pepper.

Chef's tip: I always find it easier to prepare kidneys with scissors rather than a knife. Cut away the meat in chunks and then discard the core.

Serving suggestion: Serve with a small green or tomato salad.

Freezer storage life: 3 months for the kidneys.

To defrost: Heat for 10–12min on 30%, then allow to stand for 15min.

To reheat: Reheat for 10–12min on 70%.

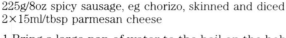

top to bottom: Devilled Kidneys with Pasta (above), Pasta with Mussels & Mushrooms (page 34), Pasta with Spicy Sausage (above)

Oven Baked Lamb with Shrewsbury Sauce

Shrewsbury Sauce traditionally requires a long simmer on the hob. In this recipe it is prepared very quickly in the microwave and served with oven-baked lamb.

Serves 4

8 shoulder cuts of lamb

Marinade
1 small onion, very finely chopped
1 clove garlic, crushed
1×15ml/tbsp freshly chopped rosemary
½×5ml/tsp salt
freshly ground black pepper
1×15ml/tbsp wine vinegar
1×15ml/tbsp olive oil
1×15ml/tbsp clear honey

Sauce
40g/1½oz butter
50g/2oz lean bacon, chopped
1 small onion, chopped
1 small carrot, peeled and chopped
2 stalks celery, chopped
25g/1oz flour
500ml/1pt boiling stock
250ml/10fl oz dry red wine
1×15ml/tbsp tomato paste
salt and pepper
1 sprig rosemary, chopped
2–3×15ml/tbsp redcurrant jelly

1 Mix together all the ingredients for the marinade and spread the mixture over the shoulder cuts. Leave for 2–3hr.
2 Melt the butter in a dish for 1–2min, add the bacon, cover and cook for 2min. Add the chopped vegetables and cook for a further 8–10min, covered, until the vegetables are soft. Stir once during cooking.
3 Stir the flour into the vegetables, then gradually add the boiling stock, wine and tomato paste. Season with salt and pepper and add the rosemary.
4 Cook for 5–6min until thickened then cook for a further 12–15min until thick enough to coat the back of a spoon.
5 Rub the sauce through a sieve and add the redcurrant jelly. Adjust the seasoning to taste.
6 Preheat the oven to gas mark 4/180°C/350°F.
7 Place the lamb in a roasting tin and cover it with foil. Bake in the preheated oven for 25–30min. Serve with the Shrewsbury Sauce.

Chef's tip: This is an excellent dinner party dish as the sauce can be prepared well in advance and reheated when required. The shoulder cuts require no last-minute attention.

Serving suggestion: Serve with Onion & Garlic Casseroled Potatoes (p71) and fresh vegetables in season. Cook the sauce in advance and reheat for 3–4min before serving. Cook the potatoes for 15min at gas mark 6/200°C/400°F, then continue cooking with the lamb at gas mark 4/180°C/350°F. Cook the vegetables in the microwave and leave covered, reheating for 2–3min, if necessary, before serving.

Freezer storage life: 3 months.

To defrost: Heat for 10–12min on 30%, then allow to stand for 20min.

To reheat: Heat for 10–12min on 70%.

Chinese-Style Stir-Fry

This recipe combines cooking in the microwave with the Chinese wok. The microwave is used to cook the rice while the other ingredients are stir-fried.

Serves 4

2 chicken breasts, approx 175g/6oz
juice ½ lemon
2×15ml/tbsp dry sherry
2×15ml/tbsp tomato purée
1×15ml/tbsp demerara sugar
small piece fresh ginger, grated or
    ½×5ml/tsp ground ginger
2×15ml/tbsp soy sauce
225g/8oz long grain rice
pinch salt
500ml/1pt boiling water
4×15ml/tbsp oil
6 spring onions, trimmed
1 green pepper, deseeded and cut into strips
125g/4oz button mushrooms, sliced
425g /15oz can baby corn cobs, drained
230g/8oz can water chestnuts, drained
50g/2oz chinese cabbage, shredded
125g/4oz peeled prawns
25g/1oz blanched almonds
125g/4oz bean-shoots
unpeeled prawns to garnish

1 Cut the chicken breasts into thin strips. Blend together the lemon juice, sherry, tomato purée, demerara sugar, ginger and soy sauce. Toss the

chicken in the marinade and allow to stand for 30min.

2 Place the rice in a bowl with a pinch of salt and add the boiling water. Cover and cook for 12–15min. Allow to stand for 5min or until required.

3 While the rice is cooking, heat the oil in the wok over a high heat. Remove the chicken strips from the marinade and cook in the wok for 5min, stirring occasionally. Add the onions, pepper strips and mushrooms and cook for a further 2–3min, stirring occasionally.

4 Add the corn cobs, water chestnuts and chinese cabbage and cook for a further 3–4min. Add the prawns and cook for a further 2–3min.

5 Place the almonds in a microwave dish and heat for 2–3min, stirring once until browned.

6 Stir the chicken marinade into the rice and add to the wok with the bean-shoots. Stir well and heat for 2–3min until piping hot. Season to taste with salt, sprinkle with the almonds and serve immediately, garnished with a few unpeeled prawns.

Serving suggestion: Serve with some mixed vegetables, microwave stir-fried. Chop 450g/1lb peeled mixed vegetables and mix with a small piece of grated fresh ginger. Heat 2×15ml/tbsp oil in a large bowl and add the vegetables. Cook, uncovered, for 8–10min, until the vegetables are cooked but still firm. Sprinkle with lemon juice, season to taste with salt and serve.

Do not freeze.

Hazelnut Stuffed Loin of Pork

The microwave is used to prepare the stuffing for this roast.

Serves 6

1×1.5kg/3lb loin of pork with kidney,
   chined and with rib bones removed
125g/4oz blanched hazelnuts
1 large onion, chopped
75g/3oz breadcrumbs
1×15ml/tbsp chopped fresh sage
salt and pepper
1 egg, beaten

1 Preheat the conventional oven to gas mark 6/200°C/400°F.

2 Remove the kidney from the pork and chop it finely, discarding the core and skin.

3 Heat the hazelnuts for 3–4min on a microwave plastic plate, until browned. Stir once during heating. Chop finely in a food processor or liquidiser.

4 Place the onion and kidney in a covered dish and cook for 4–5min, stirring once. Add the hazelnuts, breadcrumbs, sage, salt and pepper. Bind the stuffing together with beaten egg.

5 Spread the stuffing over the pork and tie loosely with string. Invert a roasting tin over the joint and turn the joint into the tin. Rub salt into the crackling and cook the pork in the preheated oven, allowing 30min per 450g/lb.

6 Remove the joint from the oven and allow to stand for 5min before carving. Meanwhile, make gravy, if required, in the microwave. Blend some gravy powder or flour with the meat juices and then add water. Heat for 3–4min, until boiling and thickened.

7 Carve the pork and serve.

Chef's tip: You cannot hope to get good crackling unless you score the fat very deeply with a sharp knife.

Serving suggestion: Serve with Roast Potatoes (p101), Apple & Aubergine Ratatouille (p70) and a fresh green vegetable of your choice. Part-cook the potatoes in the microwave, then roast with the pork. Cook the ratatouille, then transfer it to a serving dish in a water bath. Place the ratatouille in the oven to keep warm. Cook the remaining vegetable in the microwave and reheat, if necessary, for 2–3min, after the gravy has been completed.

Freezer storage life: 6 months.

To defrost: Heat for 15–18min on 30%, then allow to stand for 30min.

To reheat: Heat for 10–12min on 70%.

Chicken with Peaches & Almonds

The chicken is served in a delicious fruity sauce.

Serves 6

1 large chicken, about 2kg/4½lb, jointed
25g/1oz butter
2×15ml/tbsp olive oil
1 large onion, finely sliced
1 clove garlic, crushed
1×400g/14oz can peach slices, in
   natural juice
salt and pepper

1×5ml/tsp dried tarragon or
  1×15ml/tbsp freshly chopped tarragon
250ml/10fl oz boiling vegetable stock
demerara sugar to taste
50g/2oz split almonds

1 Heat the oil and the butter together in a large frying pan until the butter has melted. Add the chicken joints and brown on all sides, then remove the joints to a large casserole dish or bowl.
2 Add the onion and garlic to the pan and cook until the onion is browned. Add the peaches and juice, salt, pepper, tarragon and stock then bring to the boil. Cook for 2–3min then pour the sauce over the chicken joints.
3 Cover the dish and cook in the microwave for 10min on 100%. Cook for a further 20–30min at 50% until the chicken is tender.
4 Remove the chicken portions to a warmed serving dish. Liquidise the sauce in a processor or blender until smooth, adding demerara sugar, salt and pepper to taste. Pour the sauce over the chicken.
5 Place the almonds on a microwave plastic plate and cook for 3–4min, stirring once, until browned. (This can be done whilst liquidising the sauce.) Sprinkle the nuts over the casserole and serve.

Chef's tip: The chicken is browned in the frying pan to give the best possible appearance to the joints. The sauce is prepared in the pan to achieve the maximum flavour from the meat extracts and the casserole is then completed in the microwave.

Serving suggestion: Serve with conventionally boiled pasta or instant noodles. Cook a green vegetable in the microwave before cooking the chicken and reheat for 2–3min just before serving.

Freezer storage life: 3 months.

To defrost: Heat for 18–20min on 30%, then allow to stand for 10–15min.

To reheat: Heat for 10–12min on 100%, stirring once or twice.

Chicken with Celery & Water Chestnuts

Canned water chestnuts are available in most large supermarkets and are most commonly used for Chinese cookery. In this recipe they add an unusual, crisp texture to the casserole.

Serves 6 (opposite)

1 large onion, finely sliced
4 stalks celery, finely chopped
4×15ml/tbsp oil
1 large chicken approx 2–2.5kg/4½lb, cut
  into joints
225g/8oz green back bacon, chopped
375ml/15fl oz boiling chicken
  or vegetable stock
salt and pepper
1 bay leaf
2×15ml/tbsp cornflour
225g/8oz can water chestnuts,
  drained and sliced
2×15ml/tbsp single cream
chopped parsley or tarragon to garnish

1 Place the onion and celery in a large microwave covered casserole and cook for 8–10min, stirring once.
2 Meanwhile, heat the oil in a large frying pan and brown the chicken joints on all sides. Add them to the casserole, then brown the bacon in the pan.
3 Add the bacon with the seasonings and bay leaf, then pour the boiling stock over the dish. Cover and cook for 30–40min on 50% until tender. Remove the chicken joints and the vegetables to a large warmed serving dish.
4 Blend the cornflour with a little of the chicken liquor, then whisk it into the sauce. Cook for 3–4min, stirring every minute, until thickened. Season the sauce to taste, add the sliced water chestnuts and heat for a further 2min. Stir in the cream.
5 Pour the sauce over the chicken and reheat for 4–5min or place in a warm oven (gas mark 3/160°C/325°F) while cooking the accompanying vegetables in the microwave.

Serving suggestion: Serve with Leeks with Almonds (p62), and Sauté Potatoes (p61). Cook the potatoes in the microwave before starting the casserole. Transfer the chicken to a warmed oven while cooking the Leeks with Almonds.

Freezer storage life: 3 months.

To defrost: Heat for 20min on 30%, then allow to stand for 30min.

To reheat: Heat for 12–15min on 70%.

Chicken with Celery & Water Chestnuts (above), Leeks with Almonds (page 62), Sauté Potatoes (page 61)

Baked Partridge with Wild Mushroom Sauce

Serves 2

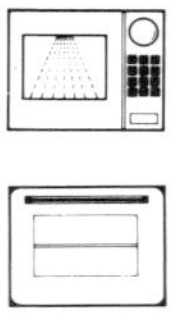

2 partridges, dressed
2 rashers back bacon
25g/1oz butter
1 shallot, chopped
225g/8oz large flat mushrooms, finely chopped
salt and pepper
pinch ground mace
2×15ml/tbsp sherry
25g/1oz flour
250ml/10fl oz milk
2×15ml/tbsp single cream
watercress to garnish

1 Preheat the conventional oven to gas mark 3/ 160°C/325°F.
2 Remove the breasts from the partridges and reserve the livers. Set aside the remainder of the carcasses for game soup (p13). Lightly beat the breasts, cut the bacon rashers in halves and place a piece of bacon across each of the partridge breasts.
3 Lightly oil or butter a piece of cooking foil and wrap round the breasts. Place on a baking sheet and cook for 30–40min in the preheated oven until tender. Whilst the partridge is cooking prepare the sauce.
4 Melt the butter in a bowl for 1–2min, add the chopped partridge livers and the shallot, cover and cook for 2–3min, stirring once. Add the mushrooms and cook covered for a further 4–5min, stirring once.
5 Add the seasonings and the sherry, then stir in the flour. Gradually add the milk then cook for 4–5min, stirring every minute, until thickened and boiling. Correct the seasoning and stir in the cream.
6 Serve with the partridge breasts.

Chef's tip: Always beat boned poultry breasts before cooking to tenderise the meat.

Serving suggestion: Serve with Roast Potatoes (p101), brussels sprouts, boiled conventionally, and Leeks with Almonds (p62) or carrots. Part-cook the potatoes in the microwave, then roast in the oven with the partridge. If serving leeks, cook the almonds in advance in the microwave. Cook the sauce and reheat for 3–4min, just before serving. Cook the leeks or carrots in the microwave and cover to keep warm while reheating the sauce.

Freezer storage life: 3 months.

To defrost: Heat for 15–18min on 30%, then allow to stand for 15min.

To reheat: Heat for 8–10min on 70%.

Vegetables, Salads & Accompaniments

The title of this chapter is somewhat vague because it is generally accepted that the cooking of vegetables is one of the finest examples of microwave cookery at its very best. Many vegetables retain a far superior colour, flavour and texture when microwaved in preference to conventional cooking.

When preparing complete meals using the microwave many people tend to cook the main part of the meal in the microwave and then be forced into cooking the accompanying vegetables on the hob. The recipes included in this chapter are for vegetables which will keep warm in the conventional oven during the final stages of meal preparation, or that accompany well other recipes included in this book and are therefore well used in meal preparation.

One or two of the recipes in this section are for main dishes where a vegetable is the main ingredient, such as Baked Patty Pan Squash (p62) or Minted Vegetable Hotpot (p64). I have also included a marmalade recipe, showing how the microwave can be used for the rapid cooking of the peel.

There are several basic rules to be observed when cooking vegetables. Root vegetables generally take 7–9min per 450g/lb and should be cooked in a covered dish with 2–3×15ml/tbsp water. Remember to stir halfway through the cooking period. Vegetables required for a purée should be cooked with approx 125ml/5fl oz water to soften them to give a smooth result. Large quantities of vegetables often cook as quickly on the hob as in the microwave, although the flavour and colour may be less satisfactory.

A basic guide for cooking vegetables will be found on p8. More comprehensive instructions will be found in your general microwave cookery book, or the manufacturers' instruction leaflet. The following recipes will further illustrate the advantages of microwaved vegetables and salads.

Sauté Potatoes

The microwave can be used to part-cook potatoes before roasting or sautéeing. For Roast Potatoes see p101.

Serves 4 (see p59)

675g/1½lb potatoes, small and evenly sized
salt
125ml/5fl oz water
50g/2oz butter

1 Peel the potatoes and place in a covered microwave dish with a pinch of salt and the water. Cook for 8–10min or until just tender, stirring once during cooking. Do not overcook.
2 Slice the potatoes thickly.
3 Heat the butter in a large frying pan, then add the potato slices. Cook for 4–5min until browned, turning once during cooking. Serve immediately.

Freezer note: Commercially frozen sauté potatoes are available but do not give a comparable result to the freshly prepared product. Even home-frozen potatoes are not the same reheated, so for that reason I do not recommend freezing this dish.

Leeks with Almonds

Leeks cook perfectly in the microwave and combine well with the crisp texture of toasted almonds.

Serves 4 (see p59)

50g/2oz split almonds
675g/1½lb leeks, trimmed, cut and washed
salt
3×15ml/tbsp water

1 Place the almonds on a microwave plastic plate and cook for 3–4min or until browned. Stir once during cooking. Leave until required.
2 Place the leeks in a covered microwave dish and add a pinch of salt. Add the water, making sure that the salt is not left on the surface of the vegetables. Cook for 6–9min, stirring once during cooking.
3 Drain the leeks and serve scattered with the almonds.

Chef's tip: The leeks may be cut into slices or left in pieces of approx 4cm/1½in. Wash them thoroughly to remove all grit and earth.

Serving suggestion: This attractive dish is useful for entertaining. Try serving with Chicken with Celery and Water Chestnuts (p58), Aubergine & Fish Lasagne (p44) or Lamb with Dill & Caper Sauce (p48).

Freezer storage life: 6 months.

To defrost: Heat for 8–10min on 50%, then allow to stand for 15min.

To reheat: Heat for 3–4min on 100%, stirring once.

Cauliflower with Mustard Sauce

A more evenly cooked result is obtained when cooking a whole cauliflower if it is boiled on the hob. This leaves the microwave available for making the accompanying sauce.

Serves 4 (opposite)

1 cauliflower, trimmed
salt
25g/1oz butter or margarine
25g/1oz flour
250ml/10fl oz milk
1–2×5ml/tsp wholegrain mustard
pepper

1 Bring a large pan of water to the boil on the hob. Score the stalk of the cauliflower deeply to speed cooking, then add to the pan and simmer for 15–20min, or until cooked.
2 Melt the butter in a microwave bowl or jug for 1–2min, add the flour and stir well. Gradually add the milk, stirring or whisking continuously.
3 Heat the sauce for 4–5min or until boiling and thickened, stirring every minute.
4 Add the mustard to the sauce, then season to taste with salt and pepper.
5 Drain the cauliflower and place on a serving plate. Pour the sauce over and serve immediately.

Serving suggestion: This complements most main dishes well – try serving with Pork with Fresh Herbs (p42), Spiced Bean Quiche (p45) or Steak & Kidney Pudding (p50).

Do not freeze as the cauliflower will collapse and become watery.

Baked Patty Pan Squash

Patty pan squashes have a soft skin and do not require peeling. The flavour is reminiscent of coconut.

Serves 2–3 (opposite)

1 patty pan squash, about 1125g/2½lb
125g/4oz rinded bacon, chopped
1 large onion, finely chopped
1 clove garlic, crushed
2 sticks celery, chopped
125g/4oz mushrooms, chopped
salt and pepper
75g/3oz cheddar cheese, grated
knob of butter

1 Preheat the oven to gas mark 5/190°C/375°F.
2 Cut a small piece from the bottom of the squash and scoop out the seeds – keep a few to put in the garden next year.
3 Place the squash in the microwave and cook for 8–10min until just softening. Remove from the microwave.
4 Place the bacon, onion, garlic and celery in a covered dish and cook for 6–8min, stirring once. Add the mushrooms and cook for a further 3–4min.
5 Season the filling with salt and pepper and stir in the cheese.

top to bottom: Minted Vegetable Hotpot (page 64), Cauliflower with Mustard Sauce (above), Baked Patty Pan Squash (above)

6 Dot the butter around the inside of the squash, then pack with the filling. Keep any juices from the filling. Replace the missing piece of squash and stand the stuffed vegetable in a small baking tin. Pour any juices from the filling over, then cover the tin loosely with foil.

7 Bake in the preheated oven for 20–25min.

Chef's tip: Squashes are becoming more readily available in supermarkets and greengrocers. They are available during the autumn months and have more flavour than the traditional marrow.

Serving suggestion: Serve as a complete meal, or with a little salad.
Do not freeze.

Minted Vegetable Hotpot

A recipe popular with vegetarians and meat-eaters alike.

Serves 6 (see p63)

900g/2lb prepared fresh vegetables in season: carrots, onions, turnips, courgettes etc
3×15ml/tbsp olive oil
salt and pepper
2–3×15ml/tbsp freshly chopped mint or 2–3×5ml/tsp dried mint
2×400g/14oz cans chopped tomatoes
125g/4oz shelled peanuts
675g/1½lb potatoes

25g/1oz butter
125g/4oz cheddar cheese, grated

1 Chop or slice the vegetables and place in a large microwave bowl or dish. Add the oil, salt, pepper and mint. Cook, covered, for 12–15min, until the vegetables are just soft.

2 Add the tomatoes and cook, uncovered, for 5–10min until well reduced and thickened.

3 Stir in the peanuts, adjust the seasoning and cover to keep warm. Preheat the oven to gas mark 6/200°C/400°F.

4 If using new potatoes, do not peel but cut into 1cm/½in slices. Cook in a covered dish in the microwave with 3×15ml/tbsp water for 10min, stirring once. If using old potatoes, peel and boil for 15–20min on the hob, then drain and cut into 1cm/½in slices.

5 Place the vegetable mixture in a large ovenproof casserole dish and arrange the drained potato slices over. Dot with the butter and sprinkle with the grated cheese. Bake for 45min until the potatoes are browned and crispy.

Serving suggestion: Serve with a crisp salad or fresh vegetables in season.

Freezer storage life: 6 months.

To defrost: Heat for 20min on 50%, then allow to stand for 15–20min.

To reheat: Heat for 10–12min on 70%.

Greek-Style Bean Ratatouille

This ratatouille makes a substantial vegetarian main course but may also be used as an accompaniment to meats cooked with herbs.

Serves 4–6 (see p43)

175g/6oz chick peas
boiling water
2×15ml/tbsp olive oil
2 large onions, finely sliced
2 large cloves garlic, crushed
1 red pepper, seeded and cut into strips
1 green pepper, seeded and cut into strips
225g/8oz courgettes, trimmed and sliced
1 large aubergine, sliced
2 lemons, grated rind and juice
1–2×15ml/tbsp freshly chopped oregano
salt and freshly ground black pepper
450g/1lb tomatoes, skinned and chopped or
   400g/14oz can chopped tomatoes
1×15ml/tbsp tomato purée
125g/4oz feta cheese

1 Place the chick peas in a large microwave dish, cover with boiling water and cover the dish. Heat for 5min then allow to stand for 1hr.
2 Drain and rinse the peas. Place in a large saucepan and cover with plenty of water. Bring to the boil and boil rapidly for at least 10min or until required.
3 Place the oil, onion and garlic in a large covered dish and heat for 3min. Add the peppers, aubergine, courgettes and lemon rind.
4 Heat the lemons for 30sec, then squeeze the fruit to remove the juice. Add the lemon juice to the casserole, cover and cook for 12–15min, stirring once.
5 Drain the chick peas and add them to the casserole with the oregano, salt and pepper, tomatoes and tomato purée. Cover and cook in the microwave for 10min on 100%, then a further 20min on 50%. Remove the lid of the casserole and, if it is necessary to reduce the sauce to thicken, cook the ratatouille, uncovered, for 8–10min on 100%. Season to taste with salt and freshly ground black pepper.
6 Preheat the grill. Cut the feta cheese into slivers and dot over the casserole. Brown the cheese under the grill for 2–3min, then serve.

Chef's tip: The chick peas are boiled on the hob at the beginning of this recipe so that the vegetables may be simultaneously cooking in the microwave, making the overall preparation time of the dish much shorter.

Serving suggestion: Serve with a tomato salad and pitta bread, warmed under the grill.

Freezer storage life: 6 months.

To defrost: Heat for 15–18min on 50%, then allow to stand for 10min.

To reheat: Heat for 12–15min on 70%.

Beetroot in Jelly

Beetroot can be cooked successfully in the microwave but I prefer the texture when they have been pressure cooked. Setting beetroot in jelly makes it much easier to serve and prevents the colour from running into other salads.

Serves 6–8 (see 67 and back cover)

450g/1lb raw beetroot, washed and trimmed
1 tablet blackcurrant jelly
375ml/15fl oz cold water

1 Cook the beetroot in a pressure cooker according to the manufacturer's instructions. Alternatively, prick the skins, then place in a microwave dish with 3×15ml/tbsp water. Cover and cook for 15–18min, stirring once during cooking.
2 Allow the beetroot to cool then peel and slice.
3 Break the jelly into cubes and place in a jug or bowl. Heat in the microwave for 1min until melted, then add 125ml/5fl oz cold water and stir until well mixed.
4 Stir the remaining water into the jelly.
5 Run an 18cm/7in microwave plastic ring mould under the cold water tap. Pour a thin layer of jelly into the bottom of the mould and place in the refrigerator until set.
6 Arrange a layer of sliced beetroot in the mould, then cover with jelly and set in the refrigerator. Continue to layer the beetroot and jelly, setting each stage in the refrigerator.
7 Chill the completed mould for 1½–2hr before serving.
8 Gently ease the jelly away from the sides of the mould with your fingers. Invert the ring onto a serving plate and carefully move the centre to allow air into the mould until the beetroot jelly drops onto the serving plate.
9 Serve sliced.

Chef's tip: Choose small, evenly sized beetroots for this recipe.
Do not freeze.

Brown Rice Salad

This salad of simple ingredients has a wonderful flavour and is a good basis for a summer buffet.

Serves 8–10 (see opposite and back cover)

450g/1lb brown rice
1litre/2pt boiling stock

Dressing:
90ml/3½fl oz olive oil
35ml/1½fl oz distilled malt vinegar
salt and pepper
1 clove garlic, crushed
1×5ml/tsp freshly chopped mint or rosemary

225g/8oz frozen petits pois
175g/6oz button mushrooms, chopped

1 Place the rice in a large microwave dish with the stock, cover and cook for 35–40min, or until the water is absorbed.
2 While the rice is cooking, place all the ingredients for the dressing in a screw-top jam jar and shake until well blended. As soon as the rice is cooked stir in the dressing. Leave to cool.
3 Place the petits pois in a covered microwave dish with a pinch of salt. Cook for 4–5min until just cooked, stirring once. Refresh the peas immediately in cold water.
4 When the rice and petits pois are cooled, mix them together with the raw chopped mushrooms. Season to taste, then refrigerate for at least 1hr. Toss the salad before serving.

Chef's tip: When cooking a large quantity of brown rice the microwave is no quicker than the hob. However, the results are much better as the grains of rice do stay separate and more fluffy.

The secret of a good rice salad is to toss the rice in the dressing as soon as it is cooked so that it can absorb the full flavour of the dressing.

Serving suggestion: This salad may also be served hot as a change from boiled rice. Add the dressing to the rice as above, but keep the rice warm by covering the dish while cooking the petits pois. Mix together the hot rice and cooked peas, then add the raw chopped mushrooms and serve.

Freezer storage life: 6 months. The salad is best served hot after freezing.

To defrost: Heat for 12–15min on 50%, then allow to stand for 10min.

To reheat: Heat for 5–6min, stirring once.

Greek Chicken Salad

Serves 6 (opposite and back cover)

125g/4oz chick peas
boiling water
5×15ml/tbsp olive oil
5×15ml/tbsp lemon juice
salt and freshly ground pepper
2 chicken quarters, skinned
3×15ml/tbsp clear honey
1×15ml/tbsp freshly chopped oregano
10 green beans, topped and tailed
2 large tomatoes, chopped
200g/7oz feta cheese, cut into small pieces
30 black olives, pitted

1 Place the chick peas in a bowl, cover with boiling water and cover the bowl. Cook for 5min, then allow to stand for 1hr. Drain and rinse the peas.
2 Place the chick peas in a large saucepan of water with a pinch of salt. Bring to the boil, then cover and simmer for 45min or until soft.
3 Mix together 2×15ml/tbsp of olive oil and 2×15ml/tbsp lemon juice. Add a little salt and pepper. Brush the mixture over the chicken portions and leave to marinade for 30min.
4 Place the chicken and the marinade in a covered microwave dish and cook for 8–10min on 70%, or until the juices run clear when the chicken is tested with a sharp knife. Allow to cool, then remove the chicken from the bone and shred.
5 Mix together the remaining olive oil, lemon juice and the honey. Add the chopped oregano and a little salt and pepper.
6 When the chick peas are soft, drain and toss in the lemon and honey dressing. Allow to cool.
7 Cut the beans into 2.5cm/1in lengths and place in a small covered bowl with 1×15ml/tbsp water. Cover and cook for 2min in the microwave at 100%, then refresh immediately in cold water.
8 Complete the salad by carefully combining the chick peas, shredded chicken, beans, tomatoes, feta cheese and olives. Season with a little salt and plenty of freshly ground black pepper. Chill for at least 1hr before serving.

Serving suggestion: This may be served as a salad in a cold buffet or as a starter. For a starter, serve on individual plates on a bed of raw, shredded spinach. Top with 1×15ml/tbsp greek yogurt. Do not freeze.

left to right: Pepper & Roquefort Quichette (page 32), Greek Chicken Salad (above), Beetroot in Jelly (page 65), Brown Rice Salad (above)

Three Fruit Marmalade

Cook the peel for marmalade in the microwave – it's much quicker than cooking conventionally and creates far less condensation in the kitchen. Boiling on the hob then allows larger quantities to be made than could be cooked completely in the microwave.

Makes approx 5kg/10lb

4 large lemons
2 sweet oranges   } approx 2.25kg/4½lb
2 large grapefruit

2litres/4pt boiling water
2.7kg/6lb granulated or preserving sugar
knob of butter

1 Wash and dry the fruit. Heat half the fruit in the microwave for 1½min, then halve and squeeze them. Repeat with the remaining fruits.
2 Remove any thick pith from the insides of the shells and tie it in a piece of clean muslin with the pips from the fruit. Place the bag in a large microwave bowl with the fruit juices.
3 Finely shred the peel and add it to the bowl with 1.5litres/3pt boiling water. Cover the bowl and cook in the microwave for 30–45min or until the peel is tender.
4 Transfer the fruit to a preserving pan, squeezing and removing the muslin bag. Add the remaining boiling water and the sugar.
5 Dissolve the sugar over a high heat, stirring regularly. Once the sugar has dissolved transfer some of the marmalade to another pan if necessary – the pan should not be more than half full to allow sufficient space for boiling.
6 Bring to the boil and cook until setting point is reached – see Chef's Tip, below.
7 Remove the pan from the heat and drop a knob of butter, cut into slivers, onto the surface of the marmalade to reduce any fruit sediment. Allow the marmalade to stand for 20min.
8 Preheat the conventional oven to gas mark ¼/ 100°C/200°F. Thoroughly wash ten jam jars and place them in the oven to warm.
9 Pour the marmalade into the warmed jars and cover with waxed discs. Cover the jars and label.

Chef's tip: The most effective way of testing for setting point is to spoon a little of the preserve onto a cold plate and place it in the refrigerator for 2–3min. When setting point is reached the preserve should form a skin and wrinkle when pushed with the finger. This applies to jams also.

Parsnips with Cinnamon & Nutmeg

This dish, based on a Flemish recipe, goes well with all roasts – try it at Christmas with the turkey. The parsnips may be kept warm in the oven for 20–30min.

Serves 4

50g/2oz butter
1 onion, finely chopped
450g/1lb parsnips, peeled and cut into
   matchsticks
salt and pepper
½×5ml/tsp nutmeg
3×15ml/tbsp red wine
1–2×15ml/tbsp demerara sugar

1 Melt the butter in a microwave-to-oven casserole dish for 1–2min. Add the onion, cover and cook for 2–3min.
2 Add the parsnips, salt and pepper, nutmeg and red wine, cover and cook for 8–10min until the parsnips are just tender, stirring once during cooking.
3 Add the demerara sugar and season to taste.
4 Serve immediately or transfer to a warm oven until required.

Freezer storage life: 6 months.

To defrost: Heat for 8–10min on 50%, then allow to stand for 10min.

To reheat: Heat for 3–4min on 100%, stirring once.

Pasta with Poppy Seeds

This unusual dish is best served as an accompaniment to grilled or roast meats as an alternative to potatoes.

Serves 4–6 (see p95)

225g/8oz small pasta tubes
salt
1×15ml/tbsp oil
1 large onion, finely sliced
1 clove garlic, crushed
2×400g/14oz cans chopped tomatoes
1×15ml/tbsp tomato paste
40g/1½oz poppy seeds
freshly ground black pepper

1 Bring a large pan of water to the boil. Add the pasta, a pinch of salt and the oil and cook for

15min, or as directed on the packet.
2 Place the onion and garlic in a large bowl and cook, covered, for 2–3min. Add the tomatoes and tomato paste, poppy seeds, salt and pepper and cook, uncovered, for 10–15min, until well reduced and thickened.
3 Drain the pasta and toss in the tomato and poppy seed sauce. Serve.

Serving suggestion: Serve with grilled meat or cold roast or any mildly herbed dishes. This is a Middle European way of cooking pasta.

Freezer storage life: 6 months.

To defrost: Heat for 12–15min on 50%, then allow to stand for 10min.

To reheat: Heat for 8–10min on 100%, stirring once.

Stuffed Tomatoes

Stuffed tomatoes make a good accompaniment to rice and pasta dishes.

Serves 4

8 large tomatoes
1 small onion, finely chopped
4 rashers rinded streaky bacon, chopped
1×15ml/tbsp freshly chopped basil
75g/3oz breadcrumbs
salt and pepper
75g/3oz emmenthal cheese, grated

1 Cut the tops from the tomatoes and reserve for use in salads. Scoop the centre from the tomatoes, reserving the seeds and discarding the cores.
2 Place the onion in a small covered dish and cook for 2min, add the bacon and cook for a further 3–4min.
3 Stir in the tomato seeds and breadcrumbs and season well, adding the chopped basil.
4 Fill each of the tomato shells with the stuffing and place them in a dish suitable for use in the microwave and under the grill.
5 Cover the tomatoes and heat in the microwave for 10min on 70%. Meanwhile, preheat the grill.
6 Sprinkle the tomatoes with the grated cheese and grill until lightly browned.

Serving suggestion: Serve with Mixed Grain Risotto (p29), Gammon Steaks with Cucumber (p42), or any pasta dish.
Do not freeze.

Apple & Aubergine Ratatouille

Perfect with pork and a delicious alternative to the traditional ratatouille.

Serves 4

1 large onion, sliced
1 red pepper, seeded and cut into strips
1 medium aubergine, halved and sliced
450g/1lb cooking apples, peeled, cored
  and sliced
salt and pepper
400g/14oz can chopped tomatoes

1 Place the prepared onion, pepper, aubergine and apple in a large covered casserole and cook for 10–12min, stirring once.
2 Season with salt and pepper and add the chopped tomatoes. Cover and cook for 10min.

3 Correct the seasoning and serve or transfer to the conventional oven to keep warm until required.

Chef's tip: Choose a well-flavoured apple for this recipe, preferably bramley or grenadier.

Serving suggestion: Serve with Pork with Fresh Herbs (p42), Hazlenut Stuffed Loin of Pork (p57) or any other pork recipe.

Freezer storage life: 1 year.

To defrost: Heat for 15–18min on 50%, then allow to stand for 10min.

To reheat: Heat for 10–12min on 100%, stirring once or twice.

Onion & Garlic Casseroled Potatoes

A variation on scalloped potatoes, delicious with many meat dishes.

Serves 4

675–900g/1½–2lb potatoes, peeled
125ml/5fl oz water
50g/2oz butter
1 large onion, finely sliced
2 cloves garlic, crushed
salt and pepper
125ml/5fl oz boiling stock
25g/1oz butter

1 Preheat the conventional oven to gas mark 6/200°C/400°F.
2 Place the potatoes in a microwave dish and add the 125ml/5fl oz water. Cover and cook for 10min, stirring once.
3 Remove the potatoes, cool slightly, then slice thickly.
4 Melt the butter in a microwave dish, add the onion and garlic, cover and cook for 3min.
5 Arrange half the potatoes in the bottom of an ovenproof dish, then spoon the onion and butter over, seasoning with salt and pepper. Top with the remaining potatoes, season and dot with the remaining butter. Pour the stock over.
6 Cover the dish and cook for 30min in the preheated oven, removing the lid for the last 15min.

Freezer storage life: 6 months.

To defrost: Heat for 10–12min on 50%, then allow to stand for 10min.

To reheat: Heat for 10–12min on 70%.

Casseroled Tomatoes

This very colourful recipe looks attractive when served with brown rice and pasta dishes.

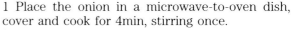

Serves 3–4

1 large onion, finely sliced
450g/1lb tomatoes, sliced
salt and pepper
1×15ml/tbsp freshly chopped tarragon or 1×5ml/tsp dried
25g/1oz wholewheat breadcrumbs
25g/1oz cheddar cheese, grated

1 Place the onion in a microwave-to-oven dish, cover and cook for 4min, stirring once.
2 Add the tomatoes, salt and pepper and tarragon. Cook for a further 6–8min, or until the tomatoes are soft, stirring once.
3 Preheat the grill.
4 Mix together the cheese and the breadcrumbs. Scatter over the tomatoes and grill until browned. Do not freeze.

German Potato Salad

This is quick to prepare if the potatoes are boiled on the hob while the bacon and onions are cooked in the microwave.

Serves 4

675g/1½lb potatoes
salt
1 large onion, sliced
125g/4oz rinded streaky bacon
1tbsp chopped chives
freshly ground black pepper
225g/8oz quark or sieved cottage cheese
chopped chives for garnish

1 Peel and thickly slice the potatoes, then boil in a pan of salted water for 10–12min until just cooked.
2 Place the onion in a microwave serving dish, cover and cook for 2–3min, add the bacon and cook for a further 3–4min, stirring once.
3 Drain the potatoes and add them to the dish with the chopped chives.
4 Carefully stir the quark into the dish and season to taste.
5 Heat, uncovered, for 3–4min on 70%, then serve immediately, garnished with a few extra chopped chives.

Serving suggestion: This is delicious served hot with sausages and mustard, or with German Sausage Loaves (p38). This salad may also be served cold.
Do not freeze.

Braised Celery

Serves 4

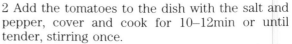

1 large onion, finely sliced
1 clove garlic, crushed
125g/4oz rinded bacon, diced
325g/12oz celery, chopped
400g/14oz can chopped tomatoes
salt and pepper
50g/2oz breadcrumbs

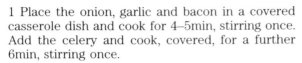

1 Place the onion, garlic and bacon in a covered casserole dish and cook for 4–5min, stirring once. Add the celery and cook, covered, for a further 6min, stirring once.

2 Add the tomatoes to the dish with the salt and pepper, cover and cook for 10–12min or until tender, stirring once.

3 Preheat the grill. Sprinkle the celery with the breadcrumbs and place under the grill to brown.

Serving suggestion: Goes especially well with fish.

Freezer storage life: 3 months.

To defrost: Heat for 10–12min on 50%, then allow to stand for 10min.

To reheat: Heat for 4–5min on 100%, stirring once.

Puddings & Desserts

A wide range of puddings and desserts may be cooked in the microwave, but by combining the microwave with the conventional cooker, it is possible to produce pies, flans and meringues baked to perfection.

Shortcrust pastry may be baked in the microwave but a crisper, shorter result is obtained from the conventional oven. The traditionally baked meringue is softer and less brittle than the microwave equivalent and retains its texture for much longer.

The recipes in this chapter really do show the best of combined microwave and conventional cooking. The microwave is used to prepare fruits and sugary fillings while pastries and meringues are baked conventionally. The microwave is also used with the pressure cooker to prepare crème caramels without the use of a water bath.

Further puddings and desserts are given in the selection of complete menus; see Fall Fruits Pie (p112), Lemon Soufflé (p116), Fig & Apple Flan (p102), Apple Crumble (p99), Pear Upside-Down Pudding (p100), Bananas & Oranges with Toasted Coconut (p114), and Chocolate Gâteau (p110).

Crème Caramels

A traditional favourite, quickly made by using the pressure cooker with the microwave cooker.

Serves 4

6×15ml/tbsp water
6×15ml/tbsp granulated sugar
375ml/15fl oz milk
2 eggs + 2 yolks
2×15ml/tbsp caster sugar

vanilla essence
few drops lemon juice

1 Heat the water in a 500ml/1pt heatproof glass measuring jug for 1min, add the sugar and stir well. Heat for a further 1–2min until the sugar is dissolved, stirring occasionally. Heat the liquid for 4–5min until golden brown.
2 While the caramel is cooking warm 4 ramekins or tea-cups in hot water and dry thoroughly. Pour some caramel into each and quickly move the dishes to coat the sides with the caramel.
3 Pour the milk into the jug in which the caramel was made and heat for 3min. Beat together the eggs and yolks, sugar and vanilla essence, then add the warm milk. Strain the custard through a nylon sieve, dividing it equally between the four caramel dishes.
4 Place the trivet, rim side down in the base of a pressure cooker and add 250ml/½pt water with a dash of lemon juice. Place the dishes on the trivet and cover with a double piece of greaseproof or silicone paper.
5 Cover the pressure cooker, bring to high pressure and cook for 3min. Allow the pressure to reduce slowly.
6 Remove the creams from the pressure cooker and allow to cool. When cold, loosen the tops of the creams and invert each one into an individual serving dish. Leave the dishes over the creams and chill well. Remove the dishes just prior to serving.

Chef's tip: Most pressure cookers are made from aluminium which tends to discolour when water is boiled in the pan. Adding the lemon juice prevents this from happening.

Serving suggestion: A light dessert, serve after any rich main course.
Do not freeze.

Raspberry Profiteroles

For a real taste of luxury in the summer, add chopped raspberries to the cream filling for profiteroles.

Serves 4 (opposite)

Pastry
50g/2oz butter
125ml/5fl oz water
8×level 15ml/tbsp flour
2 eggs, beaten

Filling
250ml/10fl oz double cream
225g/8oz raspberries

Sauce
175g/6oz plain chocolate
1×15ml/tbsp golden syrup
small knob of butter
125ml/5fl oz single cream

1 Preheat the oven to gas mark 7/210°C/425°F. Lightly grease 2 baking sheets.
2 Place the butter and water in a pan and bring to a rolling boil. Quickly shoot in the flour and beat until the mixture forms a ball, leaving the sides of the pan. Allow to cool slightly.
3 Gradually beat in the eggs to give a smooth, glossy dough of piping consistency. Place in a piping bag with a 12mm/½in tube and pipe 12 buns onto the prepared baking sheets.
4 Bake for 20–25min in the preheated oven, then slit the sides of the buns and bake for a further 15–20min at gas mark 5/190°C/375°F. Remove to a wire rack and allow to cool.
5 Whip the cream until thick but not buttery, then stir in the raspberries, carefully keeping the berries whole. Spoon the raspberry cream into the buns.
6 Break the chocolate into squares and place in a bowl with the syrup and butter. Heat in the microwave for 3–4min or until melted. Stir after 2min.
7 Stir the cream into the chocolate. Heat for 30sec, then stir until well blended. Cool before pouring over the profiteroles. Chill until required.

Serving suggestion: I always prefer to place profiteroles on individual serving plates or in sundae dishes before adding the chocolate sauce – this ensures that everyone gets their fair share.

Freezer storage life: 3 months. Freeze the chocolate sauce separately.

To defrost: Allow the buns and sauce to defrost at room temperature for 3–4hr.

Strawberry & Redcurrant Trifle

A quickly prepared, hot, summer trifle. Any left-overs may be eaten cold.

Serves 6–8 (opposite)

1 swiss roll, cut into slices
675g/1½lb strawberries and redcurrants, mixed
125g/4oz caster sugar
375ml/15fl oz milk
3 eggs, separated
25g/1oz caster sugar
2×level 15ml/tbsp cornflour
175g/6oz caster sugar

1 Preheat the oven to gas mark 7/210°C/425°F.
2 Slice the swiss roll and arrange in the bottom of a heatproof glass soufflé dish or bowl.
3 String the redcurrants and mix with the strawberries, then place the fruits in a microwave casserole dish. Add 125g/4oz sugar, cover the dish and cook for 5–6min. Spoon the fruit and juice over the swiss roll.
4 To prepare the custard, heat the milk for 3–4min in the microwave. Blend together the cornflour, 25g/1oz sugar and egg yolks in a large jug and gradually add the hot milk. Whisk well.
5 Heat the custard for a further 2–3min or until thick, whisking every 30sec. Pour over the fruits.
6 Whisk the egg whites until stiff, then gradually add the 175g/6oz caster sugar, whisking continuously. Pile the meringue carefully over the custard and fork into peaks. Be sure that all the custard is covered with meringue.
7 Flash cook in the preheated oven for 4–5min, until browned. (For a crisper meringue, cook for 15–20min at gas mark 4/180°C/350°F.)
8 Serve hot.

Chef's tip: One of the quickest ways to string redcurrants is to comb the strings over a bowl with a fork.
Do not freeze.

top to bottom: Strawberry & Redcurrant Trifle (above), Raspberry Profiteroles (above), Blackcurrant & Almond Tart (page 76)

Blackcurrant & Almond Tart

A rich summer dessert with a delicious almond pastry.

Serves 6–8 (see p75)

75g/3oz flaked almonds
175g/6oz flour
125g/4oz butter
25g/1oz caster sugar
1 egg
675g/1½lb blackcurrants
325g/12oz granulated sugar
3×15ml/tbsp arrowroot
grated rind 1 lemon
225g/8oz curd or cream cheese

1 Place the almonds on a microwave plastic plate and cook for 2–3min or until browned. Stir once during cooking.
2 Roughly grind 50g/2oz of the almonds in a blender or food processor. Place in a bowl with the flour, butter, sugar and egg. Work to a dough, rubbing the butter into the other ingredients. Wrap and chill for 30min. Preheat the oven to gas mark 5/190°C/375°F.
3 Roll the pastry out on a floured surface and use to line a 20cm/8in flan tin or sandwich tin. Prick the base of the pastry with a fork and line with greaseproof paper. Fill the pastry with baking beans and bake blind for 20–25min. Remove the baking beans and paper and cook for a further 5min.
4 Roughly string the blackcurrants and place in a large bowl with the granulated sugar. Cook for 10min in the microwave or until the fruit is soft. Stir once during cooking.
5 Rub the blackcurrants and juice through a sieve. Mix the arrowroot with a little of the blackcurrant liquid, then add the remainder with the grated lemon rind. Heat for 6min or until boiling and very thick, stirring every minute.
6 Allow to cool for 10–15min, then beat in the curd or cream cheese. Pour the filling into the pastry case and sprinkle with the remaining flaked almonds.
7 Chill for 1–2hr before serving with cream.

Chef's tip: Don't worry about topping and tailing the blackcurrants too thoroughly for this recipe – any stalks and tails will be removed when the fruit is sieved.

Freezer storage life: 4 months.

To defrost: Heat for 12–15min on 30%, then allow to stand for 30min.

Gooseberry & Elderflower Cheesecake

This baked cheesecake is less rich than many chilled cheesecakes.

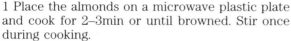

Serves 8

450g/1lb gooseberries, topped and tailed
4 heads of elderflowers
3×15ml/tbsp water

Pastry
225g/8oz plain flour
160g/5½oz butter or margarine
40g/1½oz caster sugar
1 egg yolk

Filling
50g/2oz butter or margarine
25g/1oz light muscovado sugar
1 egg, beaten
275g/10oz cream cheese
50–75g/2–3oz caster sugar

1 Place the gooseberries, elderflowers and water in a covered microwave dish and cook for 6–8min, stirring once. Remove the elderflowers and allow the gooseberries to cool.
2 Prepare the pastry by placing all the ingredients in a mixer or processor and blending together into a stiff dough. Wrap the pastry and chill in the refrigerator for 30min.
3 Preheat the conventional oven to gas mark 5/190°C/375°F.
4 Roll out the pastry and line a 20cm/8in loose bottomed tin. Prick the pastry and line with greaseproof paper. Fill with baking beans and bake blind for 20–25min in the preheated oven. Remove the beans and paper and cook for a further 5min. Reduce the oven setting to gas mark 3/160°C/325°F.
5 Cream together the butter and sugar, add the egg and the cream cheese and beat until thick and creamy. Add half the gooseberries and spoon the filling into the pastry case.
6 Bake the cheesecake in the oven for approx 1hr, until the filling is set. Allow to cool.
7 Sweeten the remaining gooseberries with caster sugar and spoon onto the filling. Chill for 2–3hr before serving.

Chef's tip: Adding a few elderflowers to gooseberries during cooking gives a flavour similar to champagne.

Freezer storage life: 6 months.

To defrost: Heat for 12–15min on 30%, then allow to stand at room temperature for 1hr.

Lemon Meringue Pie

Using the microwave to prepare the filling for this traditional favourite prevents the thick cornflour filling from burning during cooking.

Serves 6–8

Pastry
125g/4oz plain flour
50g/2oz margarine or butter
water to mix

Filling
2 lemons, grated rind and juice
3 level 15ml/tbsp cornflour
125ml/5fl oz water
125g/4oz caster sugar
2 eggs, separated
75g/3oz caster sugar

1 Preheat the conventional oven to gas mark 5/190°C/375°F.
2 Prepare the pastry by rubbing the fat into the flour until the mixture resembles fine bread-crumbs. Mix with water, then turn onto a lightly floured board and knead gently. Roll out and use to line a 20cm/8in flan dish.

3 Prick the base of the pastry with a fork, then line with greaseproof paper and fill with baking beans. Bake blind for 15–20min, then remove the baking beans and cook for a further 5–10min.
4 While the pastry is cooking, prepare the filling. Grate the rind from the lemons, then heat the fruit in the microwave for 30sec. Squeeze the lemons.
5 Mix the cornflour to a paste with the lemon juice in a bowl or jug. Add the lemon rind and water and heat for 2–3min, stirring every minute, until thickened and boiled. Shoot in the 125g/4oz caster sugar and stir well until dissolved. Allow to cool slightly, then add the egg yolks.
6 Pour the filling into the pastry case. Increase the oven setting to gas mark 6/200°C/400°F.
7 Prepare the meringue by whisking the egg whites until stiff, then gradually whisking in 75g/3oz caster sugar. Pile the meringue onto the lemon pie and bake in the oven for 10min or until the meringue is browned and set.
8 Allow to cool before serving.

Chef's tip: Heat citrus fruit until warm after grating the rinds to get the maximum amount of juice from the fruit.
Do not freeze.

Mango Meringue Pie

Mangoes are now easy to find in good greengrocers and large supermarkets. This dessert makes an unusual alternative to the ever popular Lemon Meringue Pie (see p77).

Serves 6–8 (opposite)

175g/6oz flour
125g/4oz butter
25g/1oz caster sugar
1 egg yolk
2 ripe mangoes
juice half a lemon
75g/3oz caster sugar
3 eggs, separated
175g/6oz caster sugar

1 Preheat the oven to gas mark 5/190°C/375°F. Lightly grease a 20cm/8in flan dish.
2 To prepare the pastry, place the flour in a large bowl and rub in the butter until the mixture resembles fine crumbs. Stir in the sugar and egg yolk, then bring the pastry together with your hand.
3 Lightly knead the pastry on a floured board, then roll out and use to line the prepared dish. Prick the base of the pastry case and line with greaseproof paper. Fill the case with baking beans, then bake in the preheated oven for 20–25min. Remove the paper and beans and cook for a further 5min.
4 Peel the mangoes and chop the fruit. Place the mangoes in a liquidiser or processor with the lemon juice and 75g/3oz sugar and purée. Beat the egg yolks into the mango purée.
5 Cook the purée in the microwave for 5–6min, stirring every minute. until thick enough to coat the back of a wooden spoon. Pour the filling into the pastry case.
6 Whisk the egg whites until stiff, then gradually add 175g/6oz sugar, whisking continuously. Pile the meringue into the pastry case and spread evenly over the filling. Form into small peaks with a fork.
7 Bake the meringue for 10–15min until lightly browned. Serve warm or cold.

Chef's tip: Buy mangoes when they are still firm and keep in a warm place, such as the airing cupboard, for 2–3 days, to ripen.
  To peel a mango without waste, stand the mango on its rounded end and cut through from top to bottom, allowing the knife to feel its way against the large flat stone in the centre. Repeat on the other side of the stone. Trim the skin from the remaining flesh around the stone and cut into small pieces. Score the mango flesh in the two

halves into small squares, then push upwards on the skin so that the mango almost turns inside out, and looks like a hedgehog! With a sharp knife, trim the cubes of mango from the skin.

Serving suggestion: Serve unaccompanied or with single cream.
Do not freeze.

Lemon Queen of Puddings

The lemon in this takes away much of the heavy sweetness of the traditional Queen of Puddings.

Serves 6

500ml/1pt milk
40g/1½oz butter, cut into slivers
1 lemon, grated rind and juice
125g/4oz fresh white breadcrumbs
25g/1oz caster sugar
4 eggs, separated
4×15ml/tbsp lemon curd
125g/4oz caster sugar

1 Heat the milk, butter and lemon rind together for 5min. Stir in the breadcrumbs and leave to stand for 15min.
2 Stir the lemon juice, sugar and egg yolks into the breadcrumb mixture and mix well. Pour into a large microwave to oven casserole and cook for 20–25min on 50%.
3 Allow to cool slightly, then spread with the lemon curd.
4 Preheat the conventional oven to gas mark 6/ 200°C/400°F.
5 Whisk the egg whites until stiff, then whisk in the sugar. Pile the meringue on top of the pudding. Cook for 10–15min in the preheated oven until browned.
Serve warm.

Chef's tip: Don't forget to heat the lemon in the microwave after grating the rind to get the maximum possible juice. Heat for 20–30sec until warm to the touch before squeezing.
Do not freeze.

Mango Meringue Pie (above), Smoked Fillet of Pork with Pineapple & Tarragon Sauce (page 40)

Summer Fruits Flambé

How to impress your guests!

Serves 8

225g/8oz granulated sugar
125ml/5fl oz cold water
125ml/5fl oz hot water
8 firm peaches, halved, stoned and peeled
225g/8oz raspberries
4 kiwi fruit, peeled and sliced
5×15ml/tbsp brandy
whipped cream to serve

1 Place the sugar in a large ovenproof glass jug with the cold water. Heat for 4–5min until the sugar is dissolved. Stir briskly once or twice during heating.
2 Cook the syrup for a further 8–10min or until a light golden brown colour.
3 Have the hot water ready and very carefully pour into the caramel to prevent further cooking. Heat for a further 30sec.
4 Place the peaches in a large microwave bowl and pour the caramel over. Cook for 6–8min on 70% until just tender. Allow to cool.
5 Add the raspberries and kiwi fruit to the peaches and transfer to a frying pan.
6 When required, heat the fruit over a gentle heat for 3–4min.
7 Heat the brandy for 30sec in the microwave, then ignite and pour over the fruit. Serve immediately, with whipped cream.

Chef's tip: This is a good dinner party dish as it can be prepared in advance. Reheating the fruit in a large frying pan ensures that it heats quickly and evenly and does not over-cook.

Always use a metal spoon to stir a caramel as it is then possible to check that the sugar is properly dissolved before boiling.

Serving suggestion: Ideally, the frying pan used should be copper which doubles as an attractive serving dish. Alternatively, transfer the fruit to a serving dish before adding the brandy.
Do not freeze.

Pear & Blackberry Flan

This dessert is best eaten in England during the month of September – don't pick blackberries after 1 October as the devil then turns them sour!

Pastry
175g/6oz flour
125g/4oz butter or margarine
1×15ml/tbsp caster sugar
1 egg, beaten

6 small or 4 medium pears, halved and cored
2×15ml/tbsp lemon juice
125g/4oz caster sugar
125ml/5fl oz water
2–3 cloves (optional)
50–75g/2–3oz blackberries

Custard
1 egg, separated
1 egg yolk
50g/2oz caster sugar
2×15ml/tbsp cornflour
2×15ml/tbsp flour
250ml/10fl oz milk
vanilla essence

3×5ml/tsp arrowroot

1 Lightly grease a 20cm/8in flan dish or sandwich tin. Preheat the conventional oven to gas mark 5/190°C/375°F.
2 Prepare the pastry by placing the flour in a bowl and rubbing in the fat until the mixture resembles fine breadcrumbs. Stir in the sugar, then mix to a stiff paste with the beaten egg.
3 Turn the pastry onto a floured board and knead lightly, then roll out and use to line the prepared dish or tin. Prick the base of the pastry with a fork and line the flan with greaseproof paper and fill with baking beans.
4 Bake in the preheated oven for 20–25min, then remove the paper and beans and cook for a further 5min. Allow to cool, then remove the crust and place it on a serving plate.
5 Peel the pears and coat them with lemon juice.
6 Place the sugar, water and cloves (if used) in a microwave dish and heat for 3–4min, or until the sugar is dissolved. Stir once during cooking. Add the pears, lemon juice and blackberries and cook, covered, for 8–10min, or until tender, on 70%. Allow to cool in the syrup.
7 Beat the egg yolks and sugar for the custard with a wooden spoon until pale in colour. Add the cornflour and flour and sufficient cold milk to form a smooth paste.
8 Heat the remaining milk for 2½–3min on 100%, then pour it onto the egg mixture, whisking

continuously. Heat for 2min, whisking every 30sec, until the custard is very thick and has boiled.
9 Whisk the egg white until it is stiff, then fold it into the custard with the vanilla essence. Heat for a further 1min, then pour the custard into the pastry case.
10 Remove the pear halves from the syrup and arrange them on top of the custard. Decorate the pears with the blackberries.
11 Remove and discard the cloves. Blend the arrowroot with a little of the syrup then stir it into the remainder. Heat for 2–3min, stirring every 30sec, until boiling and thickened. Spoon the glaze immediately over the pears.
12 Allow the flan to cool completely, then chill for 2–3hr before serving.

Chef's tip: Choose firm, evenly sized conference pears for this flan and arrange the halves as the spokes of a wheel in the pastry case.

Serving suggestion: Serve with single cream poured over each slice.
Do not freeze.

Minted Rhubarb Cheesecake

A baked cheesecake which has cheddar cheese in the filling for extra flavour.

Serves 8

450g/1lb rhubarb, cut into short lengths
1×15ml/tbsp freshly chopped mint
4×15ml/tbsp water

Base
75g/3oz butter or margarine
50g/2oz walnuts, chopped
50g/2oz sesame seeds
50g/2oz demerara sugar
2×15ml/tbsp rolled oats

Filling
225g/8oz cottage cheese, sieved
3 eggs, separated
50g/2oz caster sugar
40g/1½oz plain flour
75g/3oz mild cheddar cheese, finely grated
125ml/5fl oz set natural yogurt
50g/2oz caster sugar

1 Place the rhubarb, mint and water in a covered microwave dish and cook for 7–8min, stirring once. Allow to cool.
2 Melt the butter for 1–2min, add the walnuts, sesame seeds, sugar and rolled oats and mix well.

Cook the mixture for a further 1–1½min, then press into the base of a 20cm/8in loose bottomed tin. Chill until required.

3 Preheat the oven to gas mark 3/160°C/325°F.

4 Beat together the sieved cottage cheese, egg yolks, sugar, plain flour, cheddar cheese and yogurt. Add half the rhubarb and mix well.

5 Whisk the egg whites until stiff. Add the sugar and whisk again, then fold into the rhubarb and cheese mixture. Pour over the prepared base in the tin and bake for approx 1½hr in the preheated oven, until set.

6 Allow the cheesecake to cool in the oven with the door open for 30min. Remove the cheesecake and spread with the remaining rhubarb, then cool completely before chilling in the refrigerator.

7 Remove from the tin and serve.

Chef's tip: When cooking rhubarb for general use, less sugar will be needed to sweeten the fruit if a few chopped fresh angelica leaves are added during cooking.

Serving suggestion: Serve with cream.

Freezer storage life: 6 months.

To defrost: Heat for 12–15min on 30%, then allow to stand for 1hr at room temperature.

Strawberry Tartlets

Summer fruits are served perfectly in small tartlets filled with a pastry cream or confectioner's custard.

Makes 20 (opposite)

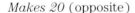

Pastry
175g/6oz flour
125g/4oz butter or margarine
1×15ml/tbsp caster sugar
1 egg yolk
water

Custard
1 egg, separated, + 1 yolk
50g/2oz caster sugar
2×15ml/tbsp cornflour
2×15ml/tbsp flour
250ml/10fl oz milk
vanilla essence

450g/1lb small strawberries

1 Preheat the oven to gas mark 5/190°C/375°F. Lightly grease 2 sheets of patty tins.

2 Rub the butter into the flour until it has the appearance of fine crumbs and add the sugar. Add the egg yolk and sufficient water, if necessary, to form a firm dough.

3 Knead the pastry on a lightly floured board, then roll out and use to line 20 of the patty tins. Prick the bases well and cook for approx 20min in the preheated oven, until golden brown. Cool on a wire rack.

4 Prepare the custard by beating the egg yolks and sugar together with a wooden spoon until pale in colour. Beat in the cornflour and flour and sufficient cold milk to make a smooth paste.

5 Heat the remaining milk in the microwave for 2½–3min, then pour onto the egg mixture. Heat for 2min, stirring occasionally, or until the mixture is very thick and has boiled.

6 Whisk the egg white until stiff, then fold into the custard. Heat for a further 1min, then add a few drops of vanilla essence.

7 Spoon a little of the custard into each tartlet. Top with strawberries and cool completely.

Chef's tip: Try to choose small strawberries that will only need to be cut into halves in order to keep the shape of the fruits.

Serving suggestion: Good for picnics and outdoor eating; these tartlets do not require cream.
Do not freeze.

Pumpkin & Raisin Pie

This recipe differs from the traditional pumpkin pie as the pumpkin remains in slices rather than being cooked as an egg-based purée.

Serves 6–8 (see p15)

675g/1½lb pumpkin flesh, peeled
75g/3oz raisins
75g/3oz demerara sugar
25g/1oz butter
350g/12oz fine wholewheat flour
pinch of salt
175g/6oz butter or margarine
warm water to mix
½×5ml/tsp ground nutmeg

1 Preheat the conventional oven to gas mark 6/ 200°C/400°F. Lightly grease a 25cm/10in pie plate.

2 Peel the pumpkin and cut into 2.5cm/1in strips,

top to bottom: Strawberry Tartlets (above), Galantine of Chicken (page 41), Pear & Whitebait Salad (page 20)

then slice across into thin wedge-shaped pieces. Layer the pumpkin in a microwave dish, alternating with the raisins and sugar. Dot with the butter, cut into slivers.

3 Cook the pumpkin for 12–15min on 70% until just softened.

4 Prepare the pastry. Place the flour and salt in a large bowl and rub in the butter until the mixture resembles fine breadcrumbs. Add sufficient water to form a stiff but manageable dough.

5 Divide the pastry into two and lightly knead each piece on a floured surface. Roll out and use one piece to line the bottom of the pie plate.

6 Drain the pumpkin and raisins using a slotted spoon and pile onto the pie plate, sprinkling the layers with grated nutmeg. Reserve the juices from the pumpkin to serve with the pie.

7 Roll out the remaining pastry and use to cover the pie. Seal the edges of the pastry together and make a hole in the top crust of the pie. Roll out any pastry trimmings and use to decorate the pie.

8 Place on a baking sheet and bake in the preheated oven for 35–40min. Serve hot with the syrup from the pumpkin and custard or cream.

Chef's tip: Pumpkins are very easy to grow if you keep a few of the seeds from a bought pumpkin. Plant in the spring as for courgettes, but one plant will be sufficient for most households as they grow very large! Tend as for courgettes.

Freezer storage life: 12 months.

To defrost: Heat for 12–15min on 50%, then allow to stand for 20–30min.

To reheat: Heat for 20–25min in the conventional oven at gas mark 5/190°C/375°F as reheating in the microwave will cause the pastry to become soggy.

Plum Ice-Cream with Brandy Snaps

Plum ice-cream is delicious!

Serves 12

Ice-cream
900g/2lb plums, washed
125ml/5fl oz water
125g/4oz soft brown sugar, or to taste
1×15ml/tbsp cornflour
2 egg yolks
250ml/10fl oz milk
500ml/1pt double cream, whisked

Brandy snaps
50g/2oz butter or margarine
50g/2oz caster sugar
2×15ml/tbsp golden syrup
50g/2oz plain flour
½×5ml/tsp ground ginger
1×5ml/tsp brandy
grated rind ½ lemon

1 Place the plums and water in a covered microwave dish and cook for 8–10min or until soft. Sieve to remove the plum skins and stones. Sweeten the purée to taste with sugar and cool.

2 Prepare a custard. Blend together the cornflour, egg yolks and a little milk. Heat the remaining milk in a jug for 3min, then pour onto the egg mixture, whisking continuously.

3 Heat the custard for 30–60sec until thickened, whisking every 15sec. Whisk into the plum purée and leave until completely cold. Fold in cream.

4 Freeze until solid, in approx 6hr, whisking occasionally.

5 While the ice-cream is freezing, make the brandy snaps. Preheat the oven to gas mark 4/180°C/350°F. Grease the handles of several wooden spoons and line 2–3 baking sheets with non-stick baking parchment.

6 Melt the butter in a large bowl for 1–2min in the microwave, then add the sugar and syrup. Beat well and heat for a further 1–2min until the sugar is dissolved, stirring every 30sec.

7 Sieve the dry ingredients into the bowl and mix to a stiff paste. Place walnut-size spoonfuls of the mixture onto the baking sheets, leaving plenty of room for spreading.

8 Bake the brandy snaps in the preheated oven for 7–10min until golden brown. Allow them to cool slightly, then remove the snaps with a palette knife and roll around the handles of the spoons. Leave until set, then transfer to a cooling rack.

9 Remove the ice cream from the freezer approx 30min before it is required. Serve in sundae dishes with the brandy snaps.

Chef's tip: If the brandy snaps harden on the baking sheets before you have rolled them all, put them back into the oven for a minute to soften.

Serving suggestion: If you have a good supply of plums, stew some in the microwave, then sieve the fruit and sweeten the purée to taste. Serve as a sauce over the ice-cream.

Freezer storage life: 6 months. Remove the ice-cream from the freezer 30min before serving.

To defrost: Allow the brandy snaps to defrost for 1–2hr at room temperature.

Baking

The microwave cooker produces excellent cakes and bread, although they are usually pale in colour unless flavoured with chocolate or coffee, or baked with dark brown sugars.

Conventional baking undoubtedly produces cakes and breads with a more appetising appearance, although the microwave can be used to great advantage in the preparation and decoration of many of the recipes.

Cakes made by the melting method, whereby butter, sugar and syrup are melted before being added to the dry ingredients, bake well in the microwave. Alternatively, the melting stage may be completed in the microwave, avoiding any danger of the rich, sugary mixtures burning over a radiant heat, and the cake may then be baked conventionally. Some biscuits made by the melting method are better baked conventionally as there is no danger of pockets of sugar burning, which can happen in the microwave if the ingredients are not perfectly blended.

In some of the following recipes the microwave cooker is used simply to prepare an icing or topping for a conventionally baked cake or biscuit. If chocolate is used in the topping, it is much easier to melt in the microwave, rather than in a double pan or a bowl in a pan of water.

Microwave baked bread is very light in texture but does not develop a crust and is pale in colour. If your preference is to bake bread conventionally, the microwave can be well used for the first rising process to speed the overall preparation time of the dough.

For a dinner party gâteau, see also the Chocolate Gâteau on p110.

Poppy Seed Cake

Serves 8–10 (see p87)

125g/4oz blue poppy seeds
200ml/8fl oz milk
225g/8oz butter or margarine
225g/8oz light muscovado sugar
3 eggs, separated
225g/8oz wholewheat self-raising flour or
   225g/8oz fine wholewheat flour +
   1×5ml/tsp baking powder
icing sugar to decorate

1 Place the poppy seeds and the milk in a jug, heat for 3min, then leave to stand for 15–20min.
2 Preheat the conventional oven to gas mark 4/ 180°C/350°F. Grease and line a 20cm/8in deep round cake tin.
3 Soften the butter or margarine in a large mixing bowl for 20–30sec, add the sugar and beat until light and fluffy, then beat in the egg yolks one at a time.
4 Beat in the flour and then the poppy seeds and milk.
5 Whisk the egg whites until stiff, then fold them into the poppy seed mixture. Spoon into the prepared tin.
6 Bake in the preheated oven for 1hr or until a skewer inserted into the centre of the cake is removed clean. Allow the cake to stand in the tin for 20min before turning out onto a wire rack to cool.
7 When cold, decorate with sieved icing sugar.

Freezer storage life: 6 months.

To defrost: Whole cake: 10min on 50%, then stand for 10–15min.
   Per slice: 2–3min on 50%, then stand for 5min.

Chocolate Coconut Crunch

Makes 16 squares (opposite)

175g/6oz plain chocolate
125g/4oz butter or margarine
1 egg, beaten
125g/4oz soft light brown sugar
50g/2oz glacé cherries, chopped
125g/4oz dessicated coconut

1 Line a 20cm/8in square shallow tin with baking parchment. Preheat the oven to gas mark 4/180°C/350°F.
2 Break the chocolate into squares and melt in the microwave for 3–4min, stirring once. Spread the chocolate in the bottom of the prepared tin.
3 Melt the butter in a large bowl for 2–3min at 100%, then add all the remaining ingredients and mix well.
4 Spread the coconut mixture over the chocolate and place in the preheated oven for 20min.
5 Mark into squares and cut when cool.

Chef's tip: Use a conventional baking parchment for this recipe and not a reusable microwave paper as this gives a far better result.

Freezer storage life: 6 months.

To defrost: Heat for 5min on 30%, then allow to defrost at room temperature for 30–45min.

Chocolate Fudge Fingers

A favourite with children of all ages, from 2 to 92.

Makes approx 24 (opposite)

150g/5oz plain flour
50g/2oz caster sugar
325g/12oz butter or margarine
1×397g/14oz can condensed milk
4×15ml/tbsp golden syrup
325g/12oz plain chocolate

1 Lightly grease and line a swiss roll tin 30.5× 23cm/12×9in. Preheat the oven to gas mark 3/160°C/325°F.
2 Place the flour and sugar in a bowl and rub in 125g/4oz of the butter, bringing the dough together to form a ball.
3 Press the shortbread mixture into the prepared tin using a palette knife to smooth the mixture over the base of the tin. Prick well with a fork.
4 Bake in the preheated oven for 5min, then lower the temperature to gas mark 2/150°C/300°F and cook for a further 30min until pale golden in colour. Allow to cool in the tin.
5 Melt the remaining butter in a large microwave bowl for 2–3min, then add the condensed milk and golden syrup. Whisk the mixture well until the butter is thoroughly incorporated into the mixture.
6 Heat for 4min or until boiling, stirring thoroughly or whisking every minute. Continue to cook for a further 3–4min until the mixture has thickened.
7 Pour the fudge evenly over the shortbread and leave to cool.
8 Break the chocolate into squares and heat in the microwave for 3–4min or until melted, stirring frequently. Spread the chocolate over the fudge mixture and leave to cool.
9 Cut into bars, and don't eat too many at once!

Chef's tip: The shortbread base for these biscuits is very thin, so spread the mixture evenly over the base of the baking sheet.

Freezer storage life: 6 months.

To defrost: These fingers are best allowed to defrost for 3–4hr at room temperature.

Glacé Fruit Cake with White Chocolate Icing

The microwave is used to prepare the unusual white chocolate icing for this cake.

Serves 12 (opposite)

250g/9oz butter
250g/9oz caster sugar
6 eggs
325g/12oz plain flour
1½×5ml/tsp baking powder
450g/1lb glacé and crystallised fruits, cherries, pineapple, ginger, papaya, etc, chopped
75g/3oz unsalted butter
225g/8oz white chocolate
2×15ml/tbsp sieved icing sugar

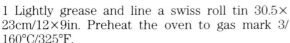

left to right: Glacé Fruit Cake with White Chocolate Icing (above), Poppy Seed Cake (page 85), Chocolate Coconut Crunch (above), Carob & Walnut Cookies (page 96), Marzipan Tea Ring (page 88), Chocolate Fudge Fingers (above)

1 Preheat the oven to gas mark 3/160°C/325°F. Grease and line a 20–22cm/8–9in round cake tin.
2 Cream together the butter and sugar until pale and fluffy, then gradually beat in the eggs.
3 Add the flour and baking powder, then fold in the chopped fruits.
4 Transfer the mixture to the prepared tin and bake in the preheated oven for 2–2½hr. Allow to cool slightly before removing from the tin and transferring to a wire rack to cool completely.
5 Cut the butter into small pieces and place in a bowl. Break the chocolate into squares and add to the butter. Heat in the microwave for 1–2min or until melting, beating well once or twice. Allow to cool slightly.
6 Add the icing sugar to the mixture and, when thick, spread over the cooled cake.

Chef's tip: Do take care when melting white chocolate as it is very high in fat and melts much more quickly than regular chocolate.

Freezer storage life: 6 months.

To defrost: Allow to defrost for 6–8hr at room temperature. The icing will melt if heated in the microwave.

Marzipan Tea Ring

Perfect for Christmas and other festive occasions, this tea ring is filled with marzipan and peel.

Serves 8–10 (see p87)

225g/8oz strong plain flour
pinch of salt
50g/2oz caster sugar
50g/2oz butter or margarine
1 egg, beaten
75ml/3fl oz milk
15g/½oz fresh yeast or
   1 sachet easy-blend dried yeast
15g/½oz caster sugar, with fresh yeast
25g/1oz butter
125g/4oz marzipan
3×15ml/tbsp apricot jam
50g/2oz chopped mixed peel
125g/4oz icing sugar, sieved
1×15ml/tsbp water, approx
40–50g/1½–2oz flaked or blanched almonds
beaten egg for brushing

1 Sieve the flour into a mixing bowl, add the salt and the sugar, then rub in the butter until the mixture resembles fine breadcrumbs. If using

dried yeast, stir it into the flour. Make a well in the centre of the flour and add the beaten egg.
2 Heat the milk for 15–20sec until tepid. If using fresh yeast, cream it with the 15g/½oz sugar and a little of the milk and add to the bowl. Add the warmed milk a little at a time and mix to a soft manageable dough, adding as much of the milk as necessary. If the mixture is a little dry, add some extra milk.
3 Turn onto a floured surface and knead until the mixture is smooth and elastic. Return the dough to the bowl, cover and heat for 15sec. Allow to stand for 5–10min, then repeat 5–6 times until the dough is doubled in size.
4 Turn the dough out onto a lightly floured surface and gently reknead. Roll out into a rectangle approx 40×30.5cm/16×12in.
5 Melt the butter for 45–60sec, then brush it over the dough. Roll out the marzipan to a strip slightly shorter than the dough and about 4cm/1½in wide, then place it on the dough, towards the lower edge.
6 Heat the jam for 1–1½ min until melted. Brush it over the dough, then sprinkle with the peel. Brush the edges of the dough with beaten egg and roll up into a long sausage shape.
7 Lightly grease a baking sheet and place the dough on it, forming it into a circle and sealing the ends together with beaten egg.
8 Cover the tea ring and leave it in a warm place for 20–30min.
9 Brush the dough with the remaining egg and make slits in the dough across the circle shape.
10 Place the dough in a cold oven, set the thermostat to gas mark 6/200°C/400°F and bake for 30–35min. Cool on a wire rack.
11 Place the icing sugar in a bowl and mix to a thick paste with the water. Spoon the icing over the tea ring.
12 Heat the almonds on a plastic microwave plate for 3min, or until browned, stirring once or twice. Sprinkle the nuts over the tea ring and serve as required.

Chef's tip: With a very rich filled dough such as this, baking from cold will help to give an extra boost to the second rising and will produce a lighter baked cake.

Freezer storage life: 4 months. Do not freeze with the icing.

To defrost: Heat for 10min on 50%, then allow to stand for 10–15min. Ice, then add the browned almonds. Leave the icing to set for at least 1hr before serving.

Battenberg Cake

When wishing to bake coloured sponges for marble cakes or battenbergs the microwave is ideal as there is no external browning of the cakes.

Makes 10–12 slices (see p91)

175g/6oz butter or margarine
175g/6oz caster sugar
3 eggs, beaten
few drops vanilla essence (optional)
175g/6oz self-raising flour
milk to mix
pink food colouring

Marzipan
1 egg
125g/4oz icing sugar
125g/4oz caster sugar
few drops almond essence (optional)
225g/8oz ground almonds

4–5×15ml/tbsp apricot jam

1 Lightly grease a shallow microwave dish approx 23cm/9in square. Cut a double thickness piece of greaseproof paper to divide the dish into halves.
2 Cream together the butter and sugar until pale and fluffy, then gradually beat in the eggs and vanilla essence, if used.
3 Fold in the flour and add sufficient milk, approx 4×15ml/tbsp, to give a very soft dropping consistency.
4 Place half the mixture in one side of the prepared dish. Colour the remainder pink and place in the opposite side of the dish. Level the mixture.
5 Cook for 6–8min on 70%, then a further 2–3min on 100%. Allow to cool slightly, then turn onto a wire rack to cool.
6 Trim the cakes, then cut each cake into two strips.
7 Place the egg and the sugars for the marzipan in a bowl over a pan of warm water on the hob. Whisk until very thick, approx 10min. Remove the bowl to the worktop. Add a few drops almond essence and fold in the ground almonds. If the mixture is very soft add a little extra sugar. Leave the marzipan to cool, covered, for 20min.
8 Place the apricot jam in a small microwave dish and heat for 45–60sec on 100%. Beat well.
9 Sandwich the strips of cake together by brushing with apricot jam. Place the same coloured pieces of cake diagonally opposite each other.
10 Roll the marzipan on a sugared board to a large rectangle that will cover the cake. Brush the marzipan with the remaining jam.
11 Wrap the marzipan around the cake and press firmly to ensure that it is well stuck. Trim the edges of the marzipan.
12 Allow the marzipan to dry for at least 1hr.
13 Serve sliced.

Chef's tip: Whisking the egg and sugars over hot water gives a pale marzipan. This is the best method to use when icing a fruit cake as a pale marzipan is far less likely to bleed through royal icing than a very yellow marzipan.

Freezer storage life: 6 months.

To defrost: Allow to defrost for 3–4hr at room temperature.

Flapjack

Using the microwave to prepare the flapjack for baking avoids any chance of the sugar mixture catching and burning during melting.

Makes 24 pieces (see p91)

250g/9oz butter or margarine
250g/9oz demerara sugar
325g/12oz rolled oats

1 Preheat the oven to gas mark 7/210°C/425°F. Lightly grease and line a swiss roll tin 30.5×25cm/12×10in.
2 Cut the butter or margarine into pieces and place in a large bowl. Heat in the microwave for 2–3min or until melted. Add the sugar and stir well.
3 Heat the butter and sugar together for approx 5min on 50% until the sugar has softened and started to dissolve.
4 Stir in the oats and mix well.
5 Spoon the mixture into the prepared tin and press down with the back of a metal spoon.
6 Bake in the preheated oven for 12–15min until golden brown.
7 Allow to cool slightly, then mark into pieces. Cut when completely cold. Store in an air-tight tin.

Chef's tip: Mixtures rich in butter and sugar, like this flapjack, cook better in the conventional oven than in the microwave as there is less chance of pockets of sugar burning.

Freezer storage life: 6 months.

To defrost: Per slice: Heat for 1–2min at 50%, then allow to stand for 5min.

Pumpkin Bread

Once you have bought or grown a pumpkin, you will welcome these recipes as good ways of using it up! The same basic recipe can be used for both sweet and savoury breads, although I prefer to use strong white flour for a sweet dough and to substitute half wholemeal flour for a savoury dough.

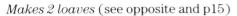

Makes 2 loaves (see opposite and p15)

Basic dough
325g/12oz pumpkin, peeled and diced
250ml/10fl oz water
900g/2lb flour
1×5ml/tsp salt
1×5ml/tsp sugar
2 sachets easy-blend yeast
3×15ml/tbsp oil
extra water for mixing

Savoury bread
50g/2oz sunflower seeds
75g/3oz cheddar cheese, grated
extra sunflower seeds for garnish

Sweet bread
125g/4oz dried figs, chopped
125ml/5fl oz water
2–3×15ml/tbsp caster sugar
beaten egg to glaze

1 Place the prepared pumpkin and the water in a covered microwave dish and cook for 8–10min or until the pumpkin is soft, stirring once during cooking. Place in a food processor or blender and work to a smooth purée – this should yield approx 500ml/1pt. Allow to cool until just tepid. Lightly oil 2 450g/1lb loaf tins or 2 baking sheets.
2 Place the flour in a large bowl with the salt, sugar and easy-blend yeast. Mix well, leaving a well in the centre of the bowl.
3 Pour the oil and pumpkin purée into the flour and mix to a workable dough, adding extra water as necessary.
4 Turn the dough out onto a floured surface and knead well until smooth and elastic. Return the dough to the mixing bowl and cover.
5 Heat for 15sec, then allow the dough to stand for 5–10min. Repeat this process 3–4 times, until the dough has doubled in size.
6 If making sweet pumpkin bread, place the figs in a small covered dish with the water and heat for 5min in the microwave during the dough's first standing period. Allow the figs to stand for 10min, drain and leave uncovered to cool. Add sugar.
7 Turn the risen dough onto a floured surface and knead lightly, working in either the sunflower seeds and grated cheese or the cooled chopped figs. Divide the dough into two and shape each piece, placing in the prepared tins or on the baking sheets. Cover and leave to rise in a warm place for 30min or until well risen.
8 While the dough is rising, preheat the conventional oven to gas mark 7/210°C/425°F.
9 Slit the tops of the savoury loaves before baking with a sharp knife and sprinkle with extra sunflower seeds. Brush the sweet loaves with beaten egg.
10 Bake for 35–40min until the base of the loaves sounds hollow when tapped. Transfer to a wire rack until cold.

Chef's tip: When making the sweet bread, the dough may become slightly sticky when the figs are being added. Extra flour may be added to the dough to stop it becoming unmanageable.

Serving suggestion: The savoury bread is a good savoury sandwich and picnic bread. The sweet bread is delicious buttered or with jam.

Freezer storage life: 6 months.

To defrost: Heat each loaf for 6–8min at 50%, then allow to stand for 10min.

Nick's Gingerbread

The microwave is used to melt the sugar, butter and syrup for this cake, which is then baked conventionally.

Makes 12 pieces (opposite)

125g/4oz margarine
50g/2oz soft brown sugar
125g/4oz black treacle
125g/4oz clear honey
125ml/5fl oz natural yogurt
2 eggs, beaten
225g/8oz fine wholewheat flour
1×15ml/tbsp ground ginger
1×5ml/tsp ground mixed spice
½×5ml/tsp bicarbonate of soda
2×15ml/tbsp icing sugar, sieved
water
1 piece stem ginger, chopped

1 Preheat the conventional oven to gas mark 2/150°C/300°F. Grease and line a 18cm/7in square or

Baking; clockwise from top: Nick's Gingerbread (above), Whisky Cake (page 93), Flapjack (page 89), Battenberg Cake (page 89), Sweet Pumpkin Bread (above)

20cm/8in round cake tin.

2 Place the margarine, sugar, treacle and honey in a large microwave mixing bowl and heat for 2–3min, stirring occasionally, until the margarine is melted and the sugar is dissolved. Cool slightly, then add the beaten egg and the yogurt.

3 Add the flour, ginger, mixed spice and bicarbonate of soda to the sugar syrup and beat well.

4 Pour the mixture into the prepared tin and bake in the preheated oven for approx 1½hr. Allow to cool slightly, then turn onto a wire rack and leave until completely cold.

5 Mix the icing sugar with a few drops of water to give a thick icing and spoon onto the centre of the cake. Sprinkle the chopped ginger over the icing.

Chef's tip: Gingerbreads mature in flavour after being stored in an air-tight tin for 2–3 days. Good luck with the self-control! This cake will keep fresh in a tin for 2 weeks.

Freezer storage life: 6 months. Do not decorate before freezing.

To defrost: Whole cake: Heat for 6min at 50%, then stand for 10–15min.

Per slice: Heat for 1–1½min at 30%, then stand for 2min.

Hot Cross Buns

Homemade Hot Cross Buns have a wonderfully fresh flavour and can be made as spicy as required.

Makes 12 large buns

450g/1lb strong plain flour
pinch salt
½×5ml/tsp ground nutmeg
1×5ml/tsp ground cinnamon
1×5ml/tsp mixed spice
75g/3oz butter or margarine
75g/3oz caster sugar
125ml/5fl oz milk and water, mixed, approx
1 egg, beaten
25g/1oz fresh yeast or
  2 sachets easy-blend dried yeast
125g/4oz currants
50g/2oz cut mixed peel
milk for brushing

Paste
40g/1½oz margarine
75g/3oz flour
6×15ml/tbsp warm water

Glaze
75ml/3fl oz milk and water, mixed
40g/1½oz caster sugar

1 Place the flour, salt and spices in a large mixing bowl and rub in the butter. Stir in the sugar and easy-blend yeast, if used.

2 Heat the milk and water for 20–30sec, until tepid. Cream the fresh yeast, if used, with a little of the liquid.

3 Beat the egg and add to the dry ingredients with the creamed fresh yeast and sufficient milk and water to give a manageable dough, adding more milk if necessary.

4 Knead the dough on a lightly floured surface until smooth. Place in a microwave bowl, cover and heat for 15sec, then leave for 5–10min. Repeat 5–6 times until the dough has doubled in size. Leaving the dough in the microwave throughout the proving process will help to speed the rising.

5 Reknead the dough lightly on a floured surface, working in the fruit and peel. Divide the dough into 12 and shape into buns.

6 Lightly grease one or two large baking sheets, place the buns on them, cover and leave in a warm place until well risen, approx 30–45min.

7 While the buns are proving, preheat the conventional oven to gas mark 7/210°C/425°F. Prepare the paste for the crosses by blending together the margarine, flour and warm water. Place the mixture in a piping bag fitted with a fine plain pipe.

8 Brush the tops of the buns with milk, then mark a cross on each bun using a small sharp knife. Pipe a paste cross over the mark.

9 Bake the buns in the preheated oven for approximately 20min, until golden brown.

10 Towards the end of the cooking period, prepare the glaze in the microwave by heating the milk and water and the sugar for 2min, stirring to make sure that the sugar is dissolved, then heating, uncovered, for a further 2–3min.

11 Remove the buns to a cooling rack, then brush with the glaze while still hot.

Chef's tip: Any yeast dough is best eaten freshly baked. To enable the buns to be cooked on Good Friday morning prepare the dough the night before, cover it and heat for 15sec in the microwave. Place the dough in the refrigerator to rise overnight. In the morning, proceed from point 5.

Serving suggestion: Serve toasted and buttered, spread with honey for a real treat.

Freezer storage life: 6 months.

To defrost: Place the buns in a ring in the microwave. Heat for 4–5min on 50%, turning the buns around half way through the defrosting time. Leave for 10min, then toast.

Whisky Cake

Serves 12 (see p91)

125g/4oz sultanas
125g/4oz raisins
125g/4oz currants
50g/2oz mixed peel, chopped
3×15ml/tbsp orange marmalade
75ml/3fl oz whisky
50ml/2fl oz milk
175g/6oz butter or margarine
175g/6oz dark brown sugar
4 eggs
1 orange, grated rind and juice
275g/10oz self raising wholewheat flour
4–5×15ml/tbsp whisky
25g/1oz flaked almonds
2–3×15ml/tbsp marmalade

1 Grease and line a 675g/1½lb loaf tin. Preheat the oven to gas mark 3/160°C/325°F.

2 Place the first seven ingredients in a bowl, cover and heat in the microwave for 5min. Allow to stand for 5min while mixing the cake.

3 Cream together the butter and sugar, then gradually add the beaten eggs and the grated orange rind.

4 Add the wholewheat flour, mixing well.

5 Heat the orange for 20–30sec in the microwave, then squeeze the juice from it and add to the cake mixture.

6 Finally, add the soaked fruit and the liquid to the cake and beat well – the mixture may appear slightly curdled but don't worry. Pour into the prepared tin and bake in the preheated oven for approx 1½hr. Allow to cool slightly before turning out onto a cooling rack.

7 Make some skewer holes in the cake and pour 4–5×15ml/tbsp whisky into the cake.

8 Place the almonds on a microwave plate or in a shallow dish and heat for 3–4min until browned. Place the marmalade in a small bowl and heat for 1–2min until melted, then sieve to remove any peel.

9 Brush the cooled cake with the melted marmalade, then scatter with the toasted nuts.

10 Wrap in foil and keep for 2–3 days.

Chef's tip: Although cake matures in just 2–3 days, it may be best to keep the fact that you are making it a secret if you want to enjoy it at its best!

Freezer storage life: 6 months. This cake will keep very well in a tin for 6 weeks or so as the whisky has a preserving effect.

To defrost: Heat for 8–10min on 50%, then allow to stand for 10–15min.

Buttermilk Rye Bread

Buttermilk and nutmeg are used to flavour this peasant-style bread.

Makes 2 loaves (opposite)

325g/12oz rye flour
325g/12oz wholewheat flour
1×5ml/tsp salt
1×5ml/tsp ground nutmeg
1×5ml/tsp sugar
15g/½oz fresh yeast or
   1 sachet easy-blend dried yeast
3×15ml/tbsp oil
125ml/5fl oz milk
250ml/10fl oz buttermilk
milk, rye flour and kibbled wheat

1 Place the flours, salt and nutmeg in a bowl. If using easy-blend dried yeast, add the sugar and yeast to the bowl.
2 Heat the buttermilk for 1min, then add sufficient milk to give 375ml/15fl oz and stir well. If using fresh yeast, cream the yeast with the sugar and a little of the milk.
3 Make a well in the centre of the flours, add the fresh yeast liquid, if used, the oil and the buttermilk. Mix to a smooth workable dough, adding extra milk if necessary.
4 Turn the dough onto a floured surface and knead for approx 10min until smooth and elastic. Return the dough to the bowl and cover with a lid.
5 Heat the dough in the microwave for 15sec, then allow to rest for 5–10min. Repeat this process four times or until the dough is doubled in size.
6 Grease 2 large baking sheets. Lightly knead the dough and divide into two. Roll each piece into a circle approx 15cm/6in in diameter and place one on each baking sheet. Cover with plastic bags or plastic film and leave in a warm place for 45min or until well risen.
7 While the bread is rising, preheat the conventional oven to gas mark 7/210°C/425°F. Brush the risen dough with a little milk and score the dough deeply into 8 segments with a sharp knife. Press some kibbled wheat into each loaf and sprinkle with a little rye flour.
8 Bake for 40–45min, until the base of each loaf sounds hollow when tapped. Cool on a wire rack.

Serving suggestion: Use warm as an alternative to potatoes with a meat casserole, or serve with cheese for a snack.

Freezer storage life: 6 months.

To defrost: Heat each loaf for 8–10min on 50%, then allow to stand for 5–10min.

Cheesy Granary Bread

Makes 2 loaves (p2)

625g/22oz granary flour
275g/10oz wholewheat flour
2×5ml/tsp salt
2×5ml/tsp molasses sugar
25g/1oz fresh yeast or
   2 sachets easy-blend dried yeast
4×15ml/tbsp oil
500ml/1pt milk and water mixed
325g/12oz cheddar cheese, grated

1 Mix together the flours, salt and sugar in a large bowl and add the dried yeast, if used. Make a well in the centre and add the oil.
2 Heat the milk and water for 1½–2min. If using fresh yeast, cream the yeast with a little of the warmed liquid, then add it to the flour. Gradually add the liquid to the flour and mix well to form a soft but manageable dough. Knead thoroughly until smooth.
3 Place the dough in a bowl and cover. Heat for 15sec, then allow to stand for 5–10min. Repeat 3–4 times until doubled in size.
4 Turn the dough onto a lightly floured surface and knead again lightly. Divide the dough into two and work 125–150g/4–5oz of the grated cheese into each piece of dough.
5 Shape the dough and place in 2 lightly oiled 450g/1lb loaf tins. Cover with plastic bags and leave in a warm place for 15–20min until risen.
6 While the loaves are rising, preheat the conventional oven to gas mark 6/200°C/400°F.
7 Sprinkle the loaves with the remaining cheese and bake in the preheated oven for 30–35min or until the base of the loaves sound hollow when tapped.
8 Remove the bread from the tins immediately and cool on a wire rack.

Chef's tip: Do not expect the loaves to rise dramatically during stage 5. The bread will also rise in the oven.

Freezer storage life: 6 months.

To defrost: Per loaf: 10–12min on 50%, stand for 10min.

top to bottom: Pasta with Poppy Seeds (page 69), Buttermilk Rye Bread (above), Lamb with Dill & Caper Sauce (page 48)

Light Rye Bread

Rye flour makes a closely textured bread. Rye flour sold in the UK is light in colour and is best mixed with some wheat flour for baking. This dough may also be used to make rolls (see p2).

Makes 1 large loaf

325g/12oz rye flour
325g/12oz strong plain flour
1×5ml/tsp salt
25g/1oz lard or margarine
1×5ml/tsp sugar
15g/½oz fresh yeast or
  1 sachet easy-blend dried yeast
375ml/15fl oz milk and water, mixed

1 Place the flours and salt in a large bowl and rub in the fat. Stir in the sugar and yeast if using easy-blend dried yeast.
2 Heat the liquid in the microwave for 45sec or until tepid. If using fresh yeast, cream it with the sugar and a little of the water. Add the yeast liquid and the water to the dry ingredients and mix to a workable dough, adding a little extra water or milk if necessary.
3 Turn the dough onto a lightly floured surface and knead well for up to 10min until the dough is smooth and elastic. Return the dough to the mixing bowl and cover with film.
4 Heat the dough for 15sec, then allow to stand for 5–10min. Repeat 3–4 times until well risen. Rye breads do not rise quite as much as wheat doughs.
5 Lightly oil a large baking sheet. Turn the dough onto a floured surface and knead lightly.
6 Shape the dough into a large oval loaf and place on the baking sheet.
7 Cover the loaf with film or a plastic bag and leave in a warm place for about 20min until well risen. Meanwhile, preheat the oven to gas mark 7/210°C/425°F.
8 Bake the loaf in the preheated oven for 35–40min or until the base of the loaf sounds hollow when tapped.
9 Place on a wire tray to cool.

Variations: To make rolls: after step 4, divide the dough into 16 pieces and shape into rolls, placing them on 2 greased baking sheets. This dough is shown as small cottage rolls on p2. These are made by dividing each portion of dough into a larger and a smaller piece and rolling each into a ball. Place the smaller ball on top of the larger, then flour your little finger and press it through the two pieces of dough to join them together. Cover the rolls and allow them to rise for 20min while preheating the oven to gas mark 7/210°C/425°F. Bake the rolls for 20min.

To make a plait as shown on p2, at step 6 divide the dough into 3 equal parts. Roll each between hands to form 'sausages'. Plait the strands together, sealing at each end.

To make Wholewheat Bread (see p2) substitute wholewheat flour for the rye flour in this recipe.

Freezer storage life: 6 months.

To defrost: Per loaf: Heat for 6–8min at 50%, then allow to stand for 5–10min.
  Per roll: Heat for 1–2min at 50%, then allow to stand for 2–3min.

Carob & Walnut Cookies

Homemade biscuits like these are really worth baking.

Makes approx 30 (see p87)

125g/4oz butter or margarine
125g/4oz light soft brown sugar
1 egg, beaten
175g/6oz self raising wholewheat flour or
  175g/6oz fine wholewheat flour +
  ½×5ml/tsp baking powder
75g/3oz walnuts, finely chopped
2×60g/2½oz carob confectionery bars or
  125g/4oz carob chips

1 Cream together the butter and sugar until pale and fluffy, then gradually add the beaten egg.
2 Add the flour and the chopped nuts and mix well.
3 Turn onto a lightly floured surface and shape the dough into a roll approx 30cm/12in long. Wrap the dough and place in the refrigerator for 1–2hr.
4 Lightly grease 2 large baking sheets and preheat the conventional oven to gas mark 6/200°C/400°F.
5 Cut the dough into rounds approx 6mm/¼in thick and place on the baking sheets, allowing room for spreading. Bake for 12min or until golden brown.
6 Allow to cool slightly, then transfer to a wire rack to cool.
7 If using carob bars, break the confectionery into squares. Place the carob in a small microwave bowl and heat for 2min. Beat well and heat for a further 30–60sec, if necessary, until melted.
8 Spread a little of the carob onto each biscuit and allow to set.

Chef's tip: The carob seed is sometimes called the locust seed and John the Baptist is reputed to have survived on it in the desert. As a confection, it is a delicious natural alternative to chocolate.

Freezer storage life: 6 months.

To defrost: Allow to defrost for 2–3hr at room temperature.

Cottage Milk Loaf

The dough may also be used to make Poppy Seed Rolls (see p2). Mixing a dough with milk gives a soft crust to the loaf – this is ideal for cottage loaves as it makes them easier to slice.

Makes 1 large loaf (see p2)

675g/1½lb strong plain flour
1×5ml/tsp salt
50g/2oz lard or margarine
1×5ml/tsp sugar
15g/½oz fresh yeast or
   1 sachet easy-blend dried yeast
375ml/15fl oz milk or milk and water, mixed
beaten egg to glaze
flour for decoration

1 Place the flour and salt in a large bowl and rub in the fat. Stir in the sugar and yeast if using easy-blend dried yeast.
2 Heat the milk in the microwave for 45sec or until tepid. If using fresh yeast, cream it with the sugar and a little of the milk. Add the yeast liquid and the milk to the dry ingredients and mix to a workable dough, adding a little extra milk if necessary.
3 Turn the dough onto a lightly floured surface and knead well for up to 10min until the dough is smooth and elastic. Return the dough to the mixing bowl and cover with film or a plastic bag.
4 Heat the dough for 15sec, and then allow to stand for 5–10min. Repeat 3–4 times until the dough has doubled in size.
5 Lightly oil a large baking sheet. Turn the dough onto a lightly floured surface and reknead gently. Cut the dough into two pieces, one approx twice as large as the other.
6 Shape the larger portion into a round and place on the baking sheet. Shape the smaller piece into another round and place on top of the first. Lightly flour a finger and press down through the two rounds of dough to bind them together.
7 Cover the loaf with film or a plastic bag and leave in a warm place for about 20min until well risen. Meanwhile, preheat the oven to gas mark 7/210°C/425°F.
8 Brush the risen loaf with beaten egg and sprinkle with a little flour. Bake the loaf in the preheated oven for 30–35min or until the base of the loaf sounds hollow when tapped.
9 Place on a wire tray to cool.

Variation: To make rolls: after step 4 divide the dough into 16 and shape into rolls, placing them on greased baking sheets. Cover and allow to rise for 20min while preheating the oven to gas mark 7/210°C/425°F. Brush the rolls with beaten egg before baking and sprinkle with poppy seeds. Bake for 20min.

Freezer storage life: 6 months.

To defrost: Per loaf: 8–10min on 50%, stand for 10min.
   Per roll: 2min on 50%, stand for 2–3min.

Complete Meals Made Easy

The art of using the microwave, in conjunction with the other cooking appliances in your kitchen, is carefully illustrated in the following suggestions for complete menus.

When preparing meals, the decision will have to be taken as to what should be cooked conventionally, either on the hob or in the oven, if a lengthy process of reheating at the last moment is to be avoided. If cooking for a large number of people, it is often best to cook at least one vegetable on the hob. In general, there is little advantage in cooking sufficient potatoes for a family in the microwave cooker.

When cooking a recipe which requires finishing in the oven or under the grill, it will be easy to cook the vegetables in the microwave cooker so that the complete course is ready at the same time. If the conventional oven is in use, it is possible to put one microwave-cooked vegetable into the warm oven until ready to serve, while cooking a second vegetable in the microwave.

The recipes in each suggested menu can all be cooked individually and offer a further, wide selection of delicious ideas for making the fullest use of your microwave cooker. Detailed plans for cooking the complete meals are also given, and the suggested menus cover everyday family eating, as well as several ideas for special occasions and celebrations.

There is a selection of recipes showing how the microwave can be used with a barbecue. A wide selection of foods can then be offered, all ready at approximately the same time. Part-cooking in the microwave ensures that all food is thoroughly cooked.

A Fish Pie for the Family

Cod & Potato Pie
Green Beans

* * *

Apple Crumble
Custard

This quick-to-prepare family meal shows all the benefits of microwave-cooked fish, and has a golden-brown topping.

Serves 4

Cod & Potato Pie

675g/1½lb potatoes, peeled
4 tomatoes, sliced
675g/1½lb filleted cod, skinned
salt and pepper
3×15ml/tbsp milk
25g/1oz butter or margarine
25g/1oz flour
250ml/10fl oz milk
2 eggs, hard-boiled
1×15ml/tbsp capers (optional)
1×15ml/tbsp freshly chopped parsley

1 Bring a large pan of salted water to the boil on the hob. Cut the potatoes into small pieces and cook for 15–20min until soft.
2 Slice the tomatoes and place in the bottom of a microwave serving dish, suitable for use under the grill.
3 Cut the cod fillet into 2–3 portions and place on

the bed of tomatoes. Lightly season the fish and pour 3×15ml/tbsp milk over. Cover and cook for 6–8min.
4 Remove the fish from the microwave. Place the butter or margarine in a jug or bowl and heat for 1–2min, until melted. Stir in the flour.
5 Gradually stir in the remaining milk, then drain the milk from the fish and add that to the sauce. Heat for 4–5min until boiling and thickened, stirring every minute.
6 While the sauce is cooking, carefully flake the fish, removing any bones. Shell and chop the hard-boiled eggs and add them to the fish and tomatoes.
7 Season the sauce to taste and add to the fish. Stir in the capers, if used, and the parsley. Heat for 4–5min on 70%.
8 Preheat the grill.
9 Drain and mash the potatoes, adding a little salt and pepper. Pile the potatoes on top of the fish, roughly decorating the top with a fork.
10 Grill for 4–5min, until the potatoes are browned. Serve immediately.

Chef's tip: Place the potato in small amounts all over the fish and then spread lightly with a fork. Alternatively, the potato could be piped around the edge of the serving dish.

Freezer storage life: 3 months.

To defrost: Heat for 12–15min on 30%, then allow to stand for 10–15min.

To reheat: Heat for 10–12min on 70%.

Green Beans

450g/1lb green beans, topped and tailed
salt
3×15ml/tbsp water

1 Cut the beans into 4cm/1½in pieces and place in a microwave casserole dish. Mix together a pinch of salt and the water and pour over the beans.
2 Cover and cook for 6–8min, stirring once during cooking.
3 Drain and serve.

Apple Crumble

675g/1½lb cooking apples, peeled,
  cored and sliced
50–75g/2–3oz sugar

Crumble
175g/6oz flour
75g/3oz butter or margarine
50g/2oz walnuts, chopped
75g/3oz demerara sugar

1 Place the apples and sugar in the bottom of a 750ml/1½pt pie dish.
2 Rub the butter or margarine into the flour until the mixture resembles fine breadcrumbs. Stir in the walnuts and the demerara sugar.
3 Spoon the crumble mixture over the apples. Cook on 50% for 12–15min until the topping is just set. Serve immediately.

Freezer storage life: 6 months.

To defrost: Heat for 8–10min on 50%, then allow to stand for 10min.

To reheat: Heat for 4–5min on 100%.

Custard

2×15ml/tbsp custard powder
2×15ml/tbsp sugar
500ml/1pt milk

1 Blend the custard powder and sugar with just sufficient milk to give a thin paste. Heat for 15–20sec, but do not allow the paste to boil.
2 Heat the remaining milk in the microwave at 100% for 4min.
3 Pour the hot milk onto the custard paste and stir or whisk well. Heat for 3–4min, or until boiling and thickened, stirring every min. Serve.

Chef's tip: Milk may be heated in milk bottles to save the washing up. Heating the custard paste in the microwave removes any taste of flour or cornflour from the custard, but do not overheat the mixture as it will become difficult to incorporate the rest of the milk and the custard may be lumpy.

To Prepare the Complete Meal
1 Prepare the Apple Crumble.
2 Prepare and cook the Cod & Potato Pie.
3 Cook the green beans while the potato pie is browning under the grill.
4 Cook the Apple Crumble while serving the main course.
5 Make the custard and serve the pudding.

A Chicken Casserole Meal

Chicken & Tomato Casserole
Boiled Rice
Peas

* * *

Pear Upside-Down Pudding

After reading through this recipe you will be able to adapt the suggested menu to include your family's favourite chicken casserole.

Serves 4

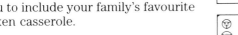

Chicken & Tomato Casserole

3×15ml/tbsp oil
1×1.5kg/3½lb chicken, cut into 4 quarters
  or 8 joints
1×5ml/tsp chilli powder
1 large onion, finely sliced
1 green pepper, seeded and cut into strips
400g/14oz can chopped tomatoes
salt and pepper

1 Heat the oil in a large frying pan. Dust the chicken pieces with the chilli powder, then brown them in the hot oil.
2 While the chicken is browning, place the onion and pepper in a microwave-to-conventional oven casserole dish, cover and cook for 4min, stirring once.
3 Add the chicken pieces to the vegetables, then stir the tomatoes into the frying pan and heat until boiling. Season with salt and pepper and pour over the chicken in the casserole dish.
4 Cover the dish and cook in the microwave for 15min while preheating the conventional oven to gas mark 3/160°C/325°F.
5 Transfer the casserole to the preheated oven for 45min.
6 Season to taste and serve.

Chef's tip: If cooking for young children, use paprika pepper in place of the chilli powder.

Freezer storage life: 3 months.

To defrost: Heat for 15–18min on 50%, then allow to stand for 10–15min.

To reheat: Heat for 10–12min on 70%.

Boiled Rice

225g/8oz long grain rice
pinch salt
500ml/1pt boiling water

1 Place the rice in a large bowl or jug and add a pinch of salt. Pour the boiling water over the rice and cover the dish.
2 Cook for 12–15min until all the water has been absorbed. Allow to stand for 5min before serving.

Peas

225g/8oz frozen peas
pinch salt

1 Place the peas in a bowl or small casserole dish and stir in the salt. Cover.
2 Cook for 5–6min, stirring once during cooking.
3 Drain and serve.

Pear Upside-Down Pudding

4 ripe pears
125g/4oz butter or margarine
125g/4oz caster sugar
2 eggs, beaten
125g/4oz self-raising wholewheat flour
3–4×15ml/tbsp milk
50g/2oz butter
4×15ml/tbsp clear honey
1 lemon, grated rind and juice

1 Lightly oil a 20cm/8in deep round microwave cake dish. Line the bottom with a circle of non-stick baking parchment.
2 Peel, halve and core the pears, then arrange them in the bottom of the dish.
3 Cream together the butter or margarine and the sugar until pale and fluffy. Add the beaten eggs, then fold in the flour. Add sufficient milk to give a very soft dropping consistency.
4 Spoon the cake mix over the pears and place the dish in the microwave, preferably on a rack.
5 Cook for 8–10min on 70%, then a further 1–2min, if necessary, on 100%. Remove from the microwave and allow to stand for 5min before turning out of the dish.
6 While the cake is standing, heat together the butter, honey, lemon rind and juice in a small bowl, for 2–3min on 100%.
7 Invert the pudding onto a serving plate and serve with the sauce poured over.

Chef's tip: A sponge to be cooked in the microwave should be much wetter than the mixture for the conventional oven. If you would usually add 2×15ml/tbsp liquid to a cake, add 4–5×15ml/tbsp for baking in the microwave.

Freezer storage life: 6 months.

To defrost: Heat for 4–5min on 70%, then allow to stand for 10min.

To reheat: Heat for 1–2min on 100%.

To Prepare the Complete Meal
1 Prepare the Chicken & Tomato Casserole as above.
2 After the chicken has been in the conventional oven for 15min, cook the rice in the microwave.
3 Prepare the Pear Upside-Down Pudding.
4 While the rice is standing, cook the peas in the microwave.
5 Set the pudding to cook while serving the casserole.
6 Prepare the sauce for the pudding, then serve.

A Roast Lamb Lunch

Roast Stuffed Shoulder of Lamb
Roast Potatoes
Turnips in White Sauce
Courgettes
Gravy

* * *

Fig & Apple Flan

This menu shows how to make the best use of the microwave in conjunction with the conventional cooker when preparing a roast.

Serves 4, with some lamb left over

Roast Stuffed Shoulder of Lamb

1.5–2kg/3–3½lb shoulder of lamb, blade bone removed
75g/3oz seedless raisins
125ml/5fl oz boiling stock
1 small onion, finely chopped
125g/4oz breadcrumbs
1×15ml/tbsp freshly chopped rosemary
salt and pepper

1 Preheat the conventional oven to gas mark 4/ 180°C/350°F.
2 Cut round the blade bone with a very sharp knife, then twist the bone sharply. Cut through the cartilage behind the joint and remove the bone.
3 Heat the raisins and stock in the microwave for 3min, covered. Allow to stand for 10min.
4 Cook the onion in a small covered dish for 2–3min, then add to the raisins with the breadcrumbs, rosemary and seasoning. The stuffing will be moist and there is no need to add any beaten egg.
5 Fill the blade bone cavity with the stuffing. Enclose the stuffing in the shoulder by trussing the shoulder with string. Alternatively, secure the lamb with wooden cocktail sticks.
6 Weigh the stuffed shoulder and roast in the conventional oven, allowing 30min per 450g/1lb.
7 Allow the lamb to stand for 5min before carving.

Chef's tip: The blade bone is easy to remove provided that you loosen all the meat from the bone. Press a thin-bladed knife flat against the back of the bone, cutting right up to the ball and socket joint. On the top of the bone there is a ridge; the meat should be scraped away from both sides of it to allow the bone to be twisted freely.

Freezer storage life: 3 months.

To defrost: Heat for 12–15min on 30%, then allow to stand for 30min.

To reheat: Heat for 15–18min on 70%.

Roast Potatoes

675–900g/1½–2lb potatoes, peeled and cut
3×15ml/tbsp water
6×15ml/tbsp oil

1 Preheat the conventional oven to gas mark 4/ 180°C/350°F.
2 Place the potatoes in a bowl with 3×15ml/tbsp water. Cover and cook for 5–8min, stirring once during cooking.
3 Drain the potatoes. Turn them in the oil and place in a small roasting tin.
4 Cook the potatoes in the preheated oven for 1–1¼hr, turning once or twice during cooking.

Chef's tip: The potatoes may be prepared as above and cooked at gas mark 6/200°C/400°F for 45min.

Turnips in White Sauce

450g/1lb baby turnips, topped and tailed
3×15ml/tbsp water
25g/1oz butter or margarine
25g/1oz plain flour
250ml/10fl oz milk
salt and pepper

1 Baby turnips do not require peeling. If using larger bulbs, peel and cut into 2–3 pieces.
2 Place the turnips in a covered microwave casserole with the water. Cook for 6–8min, stirring once. Leave covered.
3 Melt the butter in a jug or bowl for 1–2min. Stir in the flour, then gradually add the milk.
4 Heat for 4–5min, until boiling and thickened, stirring every minute. Season the sauce to taste with salt and pepper.
5 Drain the turnips, pour the sauce over and serve.

Freezer storage life: 6 months.

To defrost: Heat for 8–10min on 50%, then allow to stand for 10min.

To reheat: Heat for 4–5min on 100%, stirring once.

Courgettes

450g/1lb courgettes, trimmed
2×15ml/tbsp water
salt

1 Slice the courgettes and place in a microwave casserole dish. Stir a pinch of salt into the water, pour over the vegetables and cover the dish.
2 Cook for 5–8min, stirring once.
3 Drain and serve.

Gravy

meat juices from the roasting tin
1×15ml/tbsp gravy powder or flour
250ml/10fl oz water
gravy browning (optional)
salt and pepper

1 Pour the meat juices and a little fat from the roasting tin into a bowl or jug. Stir the gravy powder or flour into the juices, then add the water.
2 Heat for 3–4min, until boiling, stirring every minute.
3 Add a few drops of gravy browning, if required, and season the gravy with salt and pepper. Serve.

Fig & Apple Flan

Pastry
175g/6oz plain flour
pinch of salt
75g/3oz butter or margarine
water to mix

Filling
175g/6oz dried figs, roughly chopped
125ml/5fl oz apple juice
450g/1lb cooking apples, peeled, cored
   and sliced
sugar to taste, if required
50g/2oz split almonds
3×15ml/tbsp apricot jam

whipped cream to serve

1 Preheat the conventional oven to gas mark 6/200°C/400°F. Lightly grease a 20cm/8in flan dish.
2 Prepare the pastry. Place the flour and salt in a mixing bowl and rub in the butter or margarine. Add sufficient cold water to bind to a firm manageable dough.
3 Knead the pastry lightly on a floured board, then roll out and use to line the prepared flan dish.
4 Prick the base of the pastry well, then line with greaseproof paper and fill with baking beans. Bake in the preheated oven for 10min.
5 Remove the baking beans and the paper and cook for a further 5min.
6 Place the figs in a bowl with the apple juice. Cover and heat in the microwave for 5min, then allow to stand for 10min.
7 Cook the prepared apple in a covered dish for 4–5min. Add the figs and apple juice and cook for a further 4–6min, uncovered – the figs should be tender and the liquid well reduced.
8 Spoon the filling into the pastry case.
9 Place the almonds on a microwave plastic plate and cook for 2–3min until browned. Stir or toss once during cooking. Scatter the almonds over the fig filling.
10 Heat the apricot jam in the microwave for 1–2 min until melted. Brush over the almonds and the top of the flan.
11 Allow the flan to cool, then chill in the refrigerator for 1hr.
12 Serve with whipped cream.

left to right: Cod Steaks in Vine Leaves (page 105), Lamb & Vegetable Kebabs (page 105), Pork Chops (page 105), Burgers (page 104), Crispy Chicken Drumsticks (page 104)

Freezer storage life: 6 months.

To defrost: Heat for 8–10min on 30%, then allow to stand for 30min.

To Prepare the Complete Meal
Allow approx 3hr.
1 Prepare and cook the pastry case for the flan.
2 While the pastry is cooking, prepare the stuffing for the lamb.
3 Reduce the oven temperature to gas mark 4/180°C/350°F. Stuff and roast the lamb.
4 Prepare the fig and apple filling and complete the flan.
5 Prepare the roast potatoes and add to the roasting tin.
6 Whip and chill the cream. Chill the flan.
7 Cook the turnips. Make the sauce. Place the turnips in a serving dish, pour the sauce over and place in the oven to keep warm.
8 Cook the courgettes. Place in a serving dish in the oven to keep warm.
9 Remove the lamb from the oven and allow to stand for 5min before carving.
10 Make the gravy.
11 Serve the lamb, vegetables and accompaniments.
12 Serve the Fig & Apple Flan with the cream.

The Microwave and the Barbecue

All recipes serve 4

The barbecue is now a well-established part of outdoor living – pick up any summer edition of a magazine and the food feature is invariably on outdoor or al fresco eating. The microwave has a big contribution to make to barbecue
eating, especially if you are catering for a large number of people and want to feed everyone simultaneously and be certain that the food is thoroughly cooked through.

Start the food off in the microwave oven and then transfer it to the barbecue to achieve a char-grilled appearance. Cooking in relays between the microwave and the barbecue will ensure that your friends and guests do not have to wait for ages before eating.

Make sure that the barbecue is lit in plenty of time to allow the charcoal or wood to become very hot but for the fuel to be glowing rather than burning. Placing the food on the barbecue when the fuel is burning fiercely will result in fiercely

cooked (ie charred) food. Although the following recipes are all for four servings they are easily adapted for larger numbers, but do remember that not everyone will have enough room to try every dish that you cook.

Sausages

450g/1lb sausages, well pricked

Place the sausages in a dish and cook, uncovered, for 6–8min on 70%. Re-arrange the sausages once during cooking if necessary. Transfer to the barbecue and cook for at least a further 5–6min, turning occasionally, until the sausages are well browned. Serve.

Burgers

(see p103)

4×125g/4oz burgers

Place the burgers on a plate or a flat dish. Cook, uncovered, for 5min. Transfer to the barbecue and cook for at least a further 5min, turning once, until browned. Serve.

Chicken Drumsticks

(see p103)

4 drumsticks, each weighing about 125g/4oz

Cook the drumsticks, uncovered, on a rack in the microwave for 5min on 70%. Transfer to the barbecue and cook for a further 5–6min, until well browned. Turn once during cooking.

For a crispy coating
3×15ml/tbsp golden breadcrumbs
1×15ml/tbsp chopped parsley
2×15ml/tbsp cheddar cheese, finely grated
oil

1 Mix together the breadcrumbs, parsley and cheese.
2 Cook the drumsticks as above for 5min on 70%. Brush with oil, then press the breadcrumb mixture onto the chicken.
3 Continue cooking on the barbecue as above.

Cod Steaks in Vine Leaves

(see p103)

4 cod steaks, approx 125g/4oz each
8 vine leaves
salt and pepper

1 Place the cod steaks on a plate in the microwave and cook, covered, for 4–5min, or until the fish has just turned white and has the appearance of being cooked.
2 Place each of the cod steaks on a vine leaf and season lightly. Place another vine leaf over each piece of fish and wrap them individually in foil.
3 Cook on the barbecue for a further 5–8min, turning once.

Lamb and Vegetable Kebabs

(see p103)

2 neck fillets of lamb, trimmed and diced
4 lambs' kidneys, cored and halved
8 button onions
1 green pepper, cut into 8 pieces
1 red pepper, cut into 8 pieces
oil

1 Place the lamb in a small covered dish and cook for 4min, stirring once. Add the kidneys and cook for a further 2–4min. Leave covered until required.
2 Prick the onions and cook in a covered dish with the peppers for 2–3min or until just softening.
3 Thread the lamb, kidney, onions and peppers onto metal barbecue skewers, and brush with oil.
4 Cook for 10min on the barbecue, turning once.

Chef's tip: The lamb fillets may be marinated in a sauce of your choice before cooking.

Chops

(see p103)

4 lamb or pork chops
freshly ground black pepper

1 Weigh the chops and place on a microwave roasting rack. Cook for 5–7min per 450g/lb on 70%.
2 Season with pepper and cook on the barbecue for a further 8–10min for pork chops, or 5–8min for lamb chops. Turn once during cooking.

A Celebration Meal for Ten

Mushroom & French Bean Salad

* * *

Curried Petits Choux with Coriander Sauce

* * *

Grapefruit Sorbet

* * *

Venison with Juniper & Peppercorns
Spiced Apple Tartlets
Braised Red Cabbage
Courgettes

* * *

Chocolate Gâteau

This meal is for a very special occasion. Allow plenty of time for a relaxed evening and a long, leisurely meal.

Serves 10 (see p107)

Mushroom & French Bean Salad

675g/1½lb french beans, topped and tailed
225g/8oz mushrooms, sliced
3×15ml/tbsp white wine vinegar
6×15ml/tbsp oil
1 clove garlic, crushed
salt and pepper
lettuce or raw spinach to serve

1 Cut the beans into 5cm/2in lengths and place in a large bowl with the mushrooms. Cover and cook in the microwave for 4–6min, stirring once or twice, until piping hot but still crisp.
2 Place the vinegar, oil, garlic and salt and pepper in a small screw-top jar. Shake well, until blended, then pour over the beans and mushrooms.
3 Heat for a further 2–3min, uncovered.
4 Serve on a bed of lettuce or spinach.
Do not freeze.

Curried Petits Choux with Coriander Sauce

Pastry
75g/3oz butter
200ml/8fl oz water
12×level 15ml/tbsp flour, sieved
3 eggs, beaten

Filling
50g/2oz butter
1 large onion, finely chopped
1 clove garlic, crushed
1×15ml/tbsp coriander powder
1×5ml/tsp ground ginger
1×5ml/tsp ground cumin
450g/1lb monk fish tail
400g/14oz can sieved tomatoes
salt and pepper

Sauce
1×15ml/tbsp cumin seeds
grated rind of 1 lemon
500ml/1pt natural yogurt
25g/1oz fresh coriander leaves and
    stalks, finely chopped

1 Preheat the oven to gas mark 7/210°C/425°F. Lightly grease 2 baking sheets.
2 Place the butter and water in a saucepan and heat until the butter is melted and the mixture is boiling. Quickly shoot in the flour and beat until the mixture forms a ball and leaves the edges of the pan. Allow to cool slightly.
3 Gradually add the eggs and beat well to a smooth, shiny piping consistency.
4 Place the mixture in a piping bag with a 1cm/½in plain nozzle and pipe into 30 small buns on the baking sheets.
5 Bake in the preheated oven for 20min, then slit the sides of the buns with a sharp knife and cook for a further 10–15min at gas mark 5/190°C/375°F until brown and crisp. Allow the buns to cool on a wire rack.
6 Heat the butter for the filling in a microwave dish for 1½–2min. Add the onion and garlic and cook, covered, for 2min, then add the spices and cook for a further 2min.
7 Add the monk fish to the onions, cover and cook for 4min. Remove the fish from the casserole and allow to cool for a few minutes.
8 Pour the tomatoes onto the onions, add some salt and pepper, then cook, uncovered, for 10min, or until reduced and thickened.
9 Meanwhile, bone, skin and chop the fish, then add it to the sauce and heat for a further 2min, uncovered. Check the seasoning and allow to cool. Chill for 1hr.
10 Heat the cumin seeds on a microwave plate for 2min, then allow to cool.
11 Fill the choux buns with the cold fish filling and place 3 buns on each of 10 plates.
12 Prepare the yogurt sauce by mixing the yogurt with the cumin seeds, lemon rind and chopped coriander. Season to taste with salt and pepper and pour over the choux buns just before serving.

Freezer storage life: 3 months for the buns and the filling. Do not freeze the yogurt sauce. Freeze in separate containers.

To defrost: Heat the buns for 5min on 50%, then allow to stand for 30min. Heat the filling for 8–10min on 50%, then allow to stand for 10min.

Grapefruit Sorbet

3 grapefruit, grated rind and juice
2 cinnamon sticks
water
200g/7oz caster sugar
2 egg whites
extra-dry vermouth to serve

1 Grate the rind from the grapefruit into a large jug. Heat the fruit for 1½min, then squeeze the juice from them. If the fruit are very large this is easier to do by pressing the back of a 15ml/tablespoon into the flesh. Add the cinnamon sticks and sufficient water to make 750ml/1½pt.
2 Heat for 4min, allow to stand for 2–3min, then remove the cinnamon sticks and discard.
3 Add the sugar to the liquid and stir until dissolved. Strain into a large bowl through a nylon sieve and allow to cool completely.
4 Whisk the egg whites until they form soft peaks, then fold into the grapefuit syrup and freeze immediately. Stir from time to time.
5 To serve: Remove the sorbet from the freezer 30min before it is required. Spoon into bowls and pour a dash of vermouth over each serving.

Freezer storage life: 9 months.

A Celebration Meal for Ten: Mushroom & Green Bean Salad (page 105), Curried Petit Choux (above), Grapefruit Sorbet (above), Venison with Juniper & Peppercorns (page 108), Spiced Apple Tartlets (page 108), Braised Red Cabbage (page 109), Courgettes (page 109), Chocolate Gâteau (page 110)

Venison with Juniper & Peppercorns

1.5kg/3lb casserole venison

Marinade
1 large onion, sliced
3×15ml/tbsp olive oil
3×15ml/tbsp red wine vinegar
8 juniper berries
1×15ml/tbsp white mustard seeds
8 black peppercorns
8 green pepper berries
½×5ml/tsp ground white pepper
2 bay leaves
red wine

2×15ml/tbsp olive oil
2 large onions, finely sliced
450g/1lb unsmoked bacon, diced, or
    bacon pieces
50g/2oz wholewheat flour
375ml/15fl oz red wine, approx
2 bay leaves
8 juniper berries
8 black peppercorns
8 green pepper berries
½×5ml/tsp ground white pepper
½×5ml/tsp salt
1×15ml/tbsp wholegrain mustard
3×15ml/tbsp tomato paste
4×15ml/tbsp redcurrant jelly
2×15ml/tbsp demerara sugar

1 Cut the venison into large pieces and place in a casserole dish. Add the sliced onion and all the remaining marinade ingredients. Stir well, cover and leave in the refrigerator for at least 24hr, stirring occasionally.
2 Heat the oil in a large microwave bowl for 2min, add the onions, cover and cook for 4min, stirring once. Add the bacon and cook for a further 4min, stirring once.
3 Remove the venison from the marinade with a slotted spoon and add it to the casserole. Cover and cook for 8–10min, stirring once.
4 Sprinkle the flour over the venison and mix well, then add the wine and seasonings, including the mustard and tomato paste. Add remaining marinade, then red wine to cover the meat.
5 Cover the casserole and cook for 10min on 100%. Stir, then cook for 1hr on 30%. Towards the end of the hour preheat the conventional oven to gas mark 3/160°C/325°F.
6 Transfer the venison to an ovenproof casserole and cook in the conventional oven for 1–1¼hr or until the meat is tender. Remove the bay leaves.
7 Add the redcurrant jelly and the sugar, then adjust the seasoning to taste. Leave the venison in the oven until required.

Chef's tip: Ask your butcher for casserole venison. It is the whole of the forequarter of the deer, boned completely.

Freezer storage life: 3 months.

To defrost: Allow 36hr to defrost in the refrigerator, or heat for 1¼–1½hr on 30%, and allow to stand for 1hr.

To reheat: Heat for 30min on 70%, stirring once or twice, then transfer to the conventional oven at gas mark 3/160°C/325°F, until required.

Spiced Apple Tartlets

Pastry
225g/8oz flour
50g/2oz margarine
50g/2oz lard
water to mix

450g/1lb cooking apples, peeled, cored and sliced
225g/8oz redcurrants, or mixed summer fruits
8 cloves, crushed
½×5ml/tsp ground mace
125ml/5fl oz red wine
freshly ground black pepper
demerara sugar to taste

1 Preheat the conventional oven to gas mark 6/200°C/400°F. Lightly grease 2 trays of patty tins.
2 Prepare the pastry by rubbing the fats into the flour until the mixture resembles breadcrumbs. Add sufficient cold water to mix to a firm dough. Turn onto a floured board and knead lightly.
3 Roll out the pastry, stamp out with a pastry cutter, and use to line 20 of the patty tins. Prick the bases well and bake for approx 20min in the preheated oven.
4 Cool on a wire rack.
5 Prepare the filling by placing the apples, redcurrants or summer fruits, cloves, mace and red wine in a covered dish. Cook for 8–10min, covered, in the microwave. Stir once during cooking. Remove the lid and cook for a further 5min or until the juice is well reduced.
6 Add a little black pepper and sweeten the spiced fruits to taste with sugar.
7 Fill the tartlets with the spiced fruit mixture.

Freezer storage life: 6 months.

To defrost: Heat for 10–12min on 50%, then allow to stand for 10min.

To reheat: Heat for 20min in the conventional oven at gas mark 3/180°C/325°F.

Braised Red Cabbage

50g/2oz butter
900g/2lb red cabbage, finely shredded
2 large onions, finely sliced
1 large cooking apple, peeled and grated
salt and pepper
125ml/5fl oz red wine
1×5ml/tsp ground cinnamon
1×5ml/tsp ground nutmeg
2–3×15ml/tbsp demerara sugar

1 Melt the butter in a large microwave bowl for 2min. Add the cabbage and cook, covered, for 6–8min, stirring once.
2 Add all the remaining ingredients, cover the dish and cook for 18–20min, stirring once.
3 Season to taste and serve.

Freezer storage life: 6 months.

To defrost: Heat for 12–15min on 50%, then allow to stand for 10min.

To reheat: Heat for 10–12min on 100%, stirring once or twice.

Courgettes

900g/2lb courgettes, trimmed and sliced
4×15ml/tbsp water
pinch salt
butter

1 Place the courgettes in a microwave casserole dish. Mix the water with a pinch of salt and pour over the courgettes. Cover the dish.
2 Cook for 10–12min, stirring once.
3 Drain the courgettes and serve with a knob of butter.

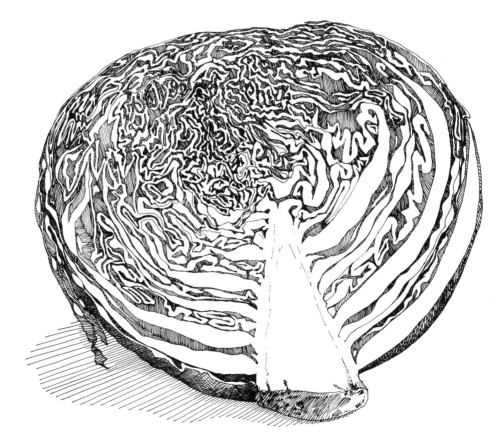

Chocolate Gâteau

75g/3oz unsalted butter
8 eggs
225g/8oz caster sugar
150g/5oz plain flour
2×15ml/tbsp cocoa powder
125ml/5fl oz double cream
7×15ml/tbsp brandy
1 lemon, grated rind and 2×15ml/tbsp juice
225g/8oz apricot jam
450g/1lb dark plain chocolate
125g/4oz unsalted butter
2×15ml/tbsp brandy
marrons glacés to decorate

1 Lightly oil a 26cm/10in microwave ring mould.
2 Cut the butter into small pieces and heat for 1½–2min until melted. Allow to cool slightly.
3 Whisk together the eggs and the sugar until very pale and thick. When the right consistency is reached, it should be possible to trickle a four-lettered word across the surface of the mixture. The first letter should still be visible when you finish writing the fourth!
4 Sieve together the flour and cocoa and heat in the microwave for 30 sec.
5 When the egg and sugar mixture is thick, gradually fold in some of the warmed flour and cocoa, then some of the cooled butter. Continue until all the flour and butter are incorporated into the cake mixture.
6 Pour the mixture into the prepared dish. Cook, preferably on a rack, for 10–12min on 70% and a further 1–2min on 100%, if required. Allow to stand for 5min then turn onto a wire rack to cool completely.
7 Whip the cream with 2×15ml/tbsp of brandy until very thick but not buttery. Heat the apricot jam with the lemon juice and rind for 30sec until the jam begins to melt, then beat well.
8 When the cake is completely cold, slice into three horizontally and place the base on a serving plate. Spread the jam over the base, then place the next layer of sponge on top. Spread with the brandied cream and top with the remaining piece of sponge, filling the centre of the gâteau with cream.
9 Make several skewer holes right through the cake and pour 3 x 15ml/tbsp brandy through the sponge.
10 Break the chocolate into squares and place in a large bowl with the unsalted butter. Heat for 3–4min, stirring once or twice, until the chocolate and the butter are melted and blended together. Beat in 2 x 15ml/tbsp brandy and leave the icing until thickened and cool.

11 Spread the chocolate over the gâteau and rough the surface with a cake comb or fork. Decorate with marrons glacés and allow to stand for 3–4hr before serving.

Prepare the Complete Meal
Much of this meal can be prepared in advance and there is very little that requires attention at the last moment.

1 1–2 days beforehand, marinade the venison, and prepare and freeze the sorbet.
2 1 day in advance, prepare and cook the choux buns and the pastry cases for the Spiced Apple Tartlets. Cool completely, then store in air-tight tins.
3 In the morning, prepare the fish filling for the choux buns. Chill. Prepare and cook the cake for the gâteau. Prepare and cook the filling for the Spiced Apple Tartlets.
4 In the afternoon, complete the gâteau and leave to stand until the evening.
5 Prepare and cook the venison 3hr before the guests are expected.
6 Fill and refrigerate the choux buns. Prepare the yogurt sauce.
7 Prepare the vegetables for the Mushroom & French Bean Salad.
8 Fill the Spiced Apple Tartlets and place in patty tins, ready for reheating.
9 Prepare and cook the red cabbage 45min before the guests are expected. Transfer to a covered serving dish and place in the oven to keep warm.
10 Cook the Mushroom & French Bean Salad when required.
11 Remove the sorbet from the freezer before beginning to eat the salad.
12 Reheat the tartlets while eating the choux buns and the sorbet.
13 Cook the courgettes while eating the sorbet.
14 Serve the venison and accompaniments.
15 Serve the gâteau.

Wine: Try serving a dry Italian wine until the end of the sorbet. The venison requires a full-bodied red wine, such as a Côtes du Rhône. Red wine kills the flavour of chocolate, so offer a sweet white German wine with the gâteau.

An Autumn Dinner: Wild Duck with Pear & Lemon Sauce (page 112), Calabrese (page 112), Fall Fruits Pie (page 112)

An Autumn Dinner

Wild Duck with Pear & Lemon Sauce
Calabrese
Baked Potatoes

* * *

Fall Fruits Pie

Serves 4 (see p111)

Wild Duck with Pear & Lemon Sauce

2 wild ducks, dressed
1 small onion, chopped
450g/1lb pears, peeled, cored and quartered
2 lemons
125ml/5fl oz dry white wine
sugar to taste

1 Preheat the conventional oven to gas mark 6/200°C/400°F.
2 Place the ducks on a rack in a roasting tin. Cook for 30min.
3 Place the onion in a covered microwave dish and cook for 2–3min. Add the pears, the grated rind and juice of 1 lemon and the wine, then cover and cook for 8–10min, stirring once.
4 After the ducks have been in the oven for 15min, baste with the juice of the remaining lemon.
5 Purée the sauce in a liquidiser or blender and add a little sugar, if required. The sauce should be sharp and tangy.
6 Allow the ducks to stand for 5min before serving with the sauce.

Chef's tip: Wild ducks are much smaller than their commercially farmed cousins, and have dark, full-flavoured meat. They should not be cooked for longer than 30min or they will become dry.

Freezer storage life: 3 months. Freeze the ducks and sauce separately.

To defrost: Heat the ducks for 10min each on 30%, then allow to stand for 10–15min. Heat the sauce for 5–6min on 50%, then allow to stand for 10min.

To reheat: Heat the ducks for 12–15min on 70%, turning once during the heating. Heat the sauce for 2–3min on 100%.

Calabrese

675g/1½lb calabrese
3×15ml/tbsp water

1 Wash the calabrese and shake dry. Trim and slit the stalks.
2 Arrange the calabrese in a shallow dish with the stalks towards the outside of the dish. Add the water, cover the dish and cook for 10–15min, rearranging the pieces once during cooking, if necessary.
3 Drain and serve.

Baked Potatoes

4 large potatoes, scrubbed
butter to serve

1 Preheat the oven to gas mark 6/200°C/400°F.
2 Prick the skins of the potatoes and place in the preheated oven, allowing 1–1½hr cooking time, depending on the size of the potatoes.
3 Serve with a knob of butter.

Fall Fruits Pie

900g/2lb fruits in season: apples, plums, pears, blackberries, damsons, etc
125g/4oz sugar
175g/6oz flour
40g/1½oz margarine or butter
40g/1½oz lard
water to mix
caster sugar
single cream to serve

1 Preheat the conventional oven to gas mark 6/200°C/400°F.
2 Prepare the fruits: peel and slice the apples and pears, wash the damsons and plums. Place the prepared fruits in a 750ml/1½pt pie dish, layered with the sugar.
3 Prepare the pastry by rubbing the margarine and lard into the flour until the mixture resembles fine breadcrumbs. Add sufficient cold water to make a stiff but manageable dough.
4 Knead the pastry lightly on a floured board, then roll out and use to cover the pie dish, allowing an extra thickness of pastry around the rim of the dish before covering with the pastry lid. Pinch the two thicknesses of pastry together and crimp the edges of the pie to give a decorative edge.
5 Cook the pie in the preheated oven for 45min. Serve hot, with cream.

Freezer storage life: 6 months.

To defrost: Heat for 10–12min on 50%, then allow to stand for 10min.

To reheat: Heat for 20min in the conventional oven at gas mark 5/190°C/375°F.

To Prepare the Complete Meal
1 Preheat the oven to gas mark 6/200°C/400°F.
2 Prepare the potatoes and place in the oven, allowing 1–1½hr cooking time, according to size.
3 Prepare the Fall Fruits Pie.
4 30min before the potatoes should be cooked, place the ducks and the pie in the oven with the potatoes.
5 Cook the Pear & Lemon Sauce.
6 Baste the ducks.
7 Cook the calabrese.
8 Liquidise and season the sauce.
9 Reheat the sauce, if necessary, for 2–3min in the microwave.
10 Serve the ducks, sauce, calabrese and baked potatoes.
11 Serve the Fall Fruits Pie with cream.

Wine: Serve a light red wine with the ducks, such as a Fleurie or a Chinon.

Calves' Liver for a Special Occasion

Calves' Liver in Brandy & Cream
Carrots with Parsnips
Brussels Sprouts

* * *

Bananas & Oranges with Toasted Coconut

Calves' liver is always a treat, and served in this cream and brandy sauce, it is sheer luxury.

Serves 4

Calves' Liver in Brandy & Cream

50g/2oz butter
675g/1½lb calves' liver, cut into thin strips
2×15ml/tbsp seasoned flour
3×15ml/tbsp brandy

1×15ml/tbsp freshly chopped sage
salt and pepper
4 slices of bread
2 rashers streaky bacon
125ml/5fl oz single cream

1 Melt the butter in a large shallow dish for 2min. Toss the liver in the seasoned flour, then add to the butter and stir well. Cover and cook for 4min, stirring once. Remove the liver from the oven.
2 Heat the brandy in a small jug or bowl for 20sec, then remove from the microwave and ignite. Pour over the liver and stir well. When the flames have subsided, add the sage and seasonings, cover the dish and cook for a further 5min on 70%.
3 Preheat the grill. Toast the bread and grill the bacon together under the grill.
4 Stir the cream into the liver and heat for a further 3min on 70%.
5 Remove the crusts from the toast and cut it into triangles. Chop the bacon.
6 Serve the liver with the toast triangles, garnished with the chopped bacon.

Chef's tip: Do not overcook the liver – it should be very soft and requires little cooking.

Freezer storage life: 2 months.

To defrost: Heat for 8–10min on 30%, then allow to stand for 15–20min.

To reheat: Heat for 8–10min on 70%.

Carrots with Parsnips

450g/1lb carrots, peeled and trimmed
450g/1lb parsnips, peeled and trimmed
4×15ml/tbsp water
salt
chopped parsley to garnish

1 Cut the carrots and parsnips into evenly sized matchsticks and place in a microwave casserole dish. Mix the water with a pinch of salt, then pour over the vegetables. Cover the dish.
2 Cook for 10–12min, stirring once during cooking. Drain and serve, garnished with chopped parsley.

Brussels Sprouts

675g/1½lb brussels sprouts
pinch salt
4×15ml/tbsp water

1 Wash and trim the sprouts and score the stalks with a sharp knife. Place the prepared vegetables in a microwave casserole dish.
2 Mix together the salt and water and pour over the sprouts. Cover the dish and cook for 12–15min, stirring once during cooking.
3 Drain the sprouts and serve.

Bananas & Oranges with Toasted Coconut

2 large oranges
50g/2oz butter
50g/2oz demerara sugar
4 large firm bananas
25g/1oz desiccated coconut
cornish ice-cream or cream to serve

1 Grate the rind from the oranges and place in a microwave serving dish, suitable for use under the grill. Remove all the pith from the oranges using a serrated knife, then cut the oranges into segments, cutting between the membranes of the oranges. Add any juice to the rind in the dish.
2 Add the butter and demerara sugar to the dish. Heat for 3–4min until the butter has melted and the ingredients are well blended.
3 Peel the bananas and slice them thickly, then add to the dish with the orange segments. Cook, uncovered, for 4min, stirring once.
4 Preheat the grill.
5 Sprinkle the bananas with the coconut and grill until the coconut is browned.
6 Serve immediately with cornish ice-cream or cream.
Do not freeze.

To Prepare the Complete Meal
1 Prepare and cook the Carrots with Parsnips in the microwave. Leave covered.
2 Bring a pan of water to the boil and cook the brussel sprouts on the hob.
3 Prepare and cook the liver.
4 Reheat the Carrots with Parsnips for 3–4min on 100%. Stir once during heating.
5 Drain the sprouts. Heat the butter and sugar for the bananas and oranges.
6 Serve the main course.
7 Quickly cook the bananas and oranges and serve immediately.

Wine: Serve a full bodied white wine made from the chardonnay grape. The Australian and New Zealand chardonnays are well worth trying.

A Celebration Meal for 6

Pâté du Maison

* * *

Stuffed Salmon en Croûte with Hollandaise Sauce
Courgettes with Sesame Seeds
Cauliflower with Tomato Sauce

* * *

Lemon Soufflé

Serves 6 (see front cover)

Pâté du Maison

450g/1lb chicken livers
125g/4oz butter
1 large onion, chopped
2 cloves garlic, crushed
1×10ml/dsp freshly chopped thyme or
⅟₂×5ml/tsp dried (optional)
2×15ml/tbsp brandy
salt and freshly ground black pepper
75g/3oz unsalted butter
peppercorns to garnish

1 If using frozen livers, remove them from their containers and place in a microwave dish. Heat for 8–10min on 30%, then leave for 10min.
2 Trim the livers and chop them roughly.
3 Melt the butter in a large microwave dish for 2–3min, add the onion and garlic and cook, covered, for 3min. Add the livers and the thyme and cook for a further 3min, covered. Stir once during cooking.
4 Remove the dish from the microwave and leave covered.
5 Heat the brandy in a small glass or jug for 20–30sec, remove from the microwave and ignite. Pour the brandy over the chicken livers and wait for the flames to subside.
6 Cover the dish and cook for a further 5min at 50%.
7 Allow the livers to cool slightly, then process or liquidise the mixture to a smooth paste. Season to taste with salt and black pepper.
8 Divide the pâté between 6 ramekins and allow to cool.
9 Heat the unsalted butter for 1–2min. Carefully spoon the butter into the ramekins.
10 Garnish with the peppercorns, then chill the pâtés for at least 2hr, or until required.

11 Serve the pâté with a small salad garnish and biscuits, or melba toast (p21).

Chef's tip: The pâté can be made well in advance of the meal.

Freezer storage life: 3 months.

To defrost: Allow to defrost for 4–5hr in the refrigerator.

Baked Suffed Salmon en Croûte

1×900–1125g/2–2½lb salmon, cleaned
75g/3oz cashew nuts
25g/1oz butter
1 small onion, finely chopped
75g/3oz wholewheat breadcrumbs
1×15ml/tbsp freshly chopped chervil
salt and pepper
1 egg, beaten
400g/14 oz packet frozen puff pastry, defrosted
1×15ml/tbsp semolina
1 egg, beaten

1 Remove the backbone from the salmon. Slit down the belly of the salmon to the tail and place the fish on a board. Press along the backbone with your thumbs, flattening the fish onto the board. Turn the salmon over and remove the bone. By carefully cutting through the bone it is possible to keep the head and tail attached to the fish if required for presentation.
2 Place the nuts on a microwave plastic plate and heat for 3–4min, stirring once or twice, until browned. Grind finely in a liquidiser or processor.
3 Melt the butter for 1min, add the onion, cover and cook for 2–3min. Add the nuts, breadcrumbs, chervil and seasonings and bind the stuffing together with the beaten egg.
4 Fill the salmon with the stuffing. Place the fish on a large flat plate and cover the tail end with a smooth piece of cooking foil. If you have left the head on, cover that with a small piece of foil also.
5 Cook the salmon, uncovered, for 10min on 50%.
6 Meanwhile, roll out the pastry to a rectangle large enough to wrap around the fish – the head and tail can be left protruding from the pastry.
7 Lightly oil a large baking sheet. Preheat the oven to gas mark 7/210°C/425°F.
8 Remove the salmon from the microwave and discard the foil. Carefully remove the skin from the upper side of the salmon, then invert the fish into the middle of the pastry. Remove the remaining skin.
9 Sprinkle the semolina over the salmon. Brush the pastry with the beaten egg, then wrap the salmon in the pastry.
10 Place the salmon on the baking sheet so that the pastry seam is underneath the fish.
11 Brush the pastry with the remaining egg and mark the shape of fish scales with a sharp knife.
12 Cook in the preheated oven for 20–25min, until the pastry is golden brown.
13 Serve sliced, with the Hollandaise Sauce.

Chef's tip: In some microwave cookers with turntables, the salmon may have to be slightly curved to fit onto the turntable. The salmon may be prepared to the end of stage 9, then covered and placed in the refrigerator until required. The semolina is used to absorb any moisture from the fish, to prevent the pastry from becoming soggy.

Freezer storage life: 3 months. Do not freeze if the salmon has previously been frozen.

To defrost: Heat for 10min on 30%, then leave to defrost for 2hr at room temperature.

To reheat: Reheat in slices in the conventional oven at gas mark 5/190°C/375°F. Reheating in the microwave would cause the pastry to become soggy.

Hollandaise Sauce

125g/4oz butter
2×15ml/tbsp white wine vinegar
salt and pepper
4 egg yolks

1 Melt the butter in a large jug for 1½–2min, then whisk in the remaining ingredients.
2 Heat for 30–45sec, whisking every 15sec, until thickened and glossy. Serve immediately with the salmon.

Chef's tip: If your microwave cooker has dial controls, rather than touch pads, the sauce should be cooked for 1–2min on 50%, stirring every 30sec. The stirring and timing of this sauce is very critical. Make the sauce just before serving as it is not easily kept warm.
Do not freeze.

Courgettes with Sesame Seeds

675g/1½lb courgettes, trimmed and sliced
salt
3×15ml/tbsp water
25g/1oz sesame seeds

1 Place the courgettes in a microwave casserole dish. Mix a pinch of salt with the water and pour over the courgettes. Cover the dish.
2 Cook for 8–10min, stirring once.
3 Drain the courgettes and add the sesame seeds. Serve.

Cauliflower with Tomato Sauce

675g/1½ lb prepared cauliflower florets
1 small onion, chopped
400g/14oz can chopped tomatoes
salt and pepper

1 Bring a large pan of salted water to the boil, add the cauliflower florets and simmer for 12–15min.
2 Cook the onion in a covered dish in the microwave for 2–3min. Add the tomatoes and cook, uncovered, for 8–10min, until thick. Season to taste with salt and pepper.
3 Drain the cauliflower and serve with the tomato sauce.

Lemon Soufflé

4 large lemons
6 eggs, separated
175g/6oz caster sugar
5×15ml/tbsp water
2×15ml/tbsp powdered gelatine
250ml/10fl oz double cream
50g/2oz almonds, chopped
sliced kiwi fruit to decorate

1 Make a greaseproof collar for a 1 litre/1½–2pt soufflé dish and tie it firmly in position with string.
2 Grate the rinds from the lemons into a large bowl. Heat the fruit for 1min, then squeeze the juice from them. Add the juice, sugar and egg yolks to the grated rind.
3 Whisk the mixture over a pan of warm water for about 10min until the mixture is pale and thick enough to coat the back of a wooden spoon.
4 Place the water in a small bowl and heat in the microwave for 30sec. Add the gelatine and stir well. Heat for a further 15sec, if necessary, until the gelatine is completely dissolved.
5 Stir 3×15ml/tbsp of the lemon mixture into the gelatine, then whisk it into the lemon mixture.
6 Chill until thick – about 30min. Scrape the mixture from the sides of the bowl and stir once or twice during this period.

7 Whip the cream until thick, and stiffly beat the egg whites.

8 Fold the cream and egg whites into the lemon mixture, then pour the soufflé into the prepared dish.

9 Place the soufflé in the refrigerator for 2–3hr, or until set.

10 Remove the greaseproof collar from the dish and roll the edge of the soufflé in the chopped almonds. Decorate with slices of kiwi fruit before serving.

Chef's tip: If you have very juicy lemons you may find that the egg mixture at stage 3 separates slightly. This will be overcome if you scrape down and mix the pudding thoroughly.

If the lemon mixture sets too much before the cream is added, it may be heated in the microwave for 15–30sec, then beaten well to obtain the correct consistency.

Do not freeze.

To Prepare the Complete Meal

1 Prepare and chill the soufflé.

2 Prepare and chill the pâté. If serving melba toasts, these may be cooked, cooled, then stored in an air-tight tin.

3 Prepare the sauce for the cauliflower and allow to cool.

4 Prepare the salmon to the end of stage 9. Remove from the refrigerator 30min before cooking. Preheat the oven.

5 Cook the salmon.

6 Cook the cauliflower on the hob.

7 Cook the courgettes in the microwave. Place in a serving dish in the oven to keep warm.

8 Serve the pâté.

9 Reheat the tomato sauce for 3–4min in the microwave. Place the cauliflower and tomato sauce in a serving dish in the oven to keep warm.

10 Prepare and cook the Hollandaise Sauce.

11 Serve the salmon, sauce and vegetables.

12 Serve the soufflé.

Wine: Serve a well-chilled, medium-to-dry white wine with this meal. A slightly sparkling wine would complement the salmon well.

Index

Numbers in italic refer to illustrations